How Far? How Fast?

David Johnson and **John Nicholson**

Series editor
Fred Webber

D0248768

CAMBRIDGE
UNIVERSITY PRESS

PUBLISHED BY THE PRESS SYNDICATE OF THE UNIVERSITY OF CAMBRIDGE
The Pitt Building, Trumpington Street, Cambridge CB2 1RP, United Kingdom

CAMBRIDGE UNIVERSITY PRESS
The Edinburgh Building, Cambridge CB2 2RU, United Kingdom
40 West 20th Street, New York, NY 10011–4211, USA
10 Stamford Road, Oakleigh, Melbourne 3166, Australia

First published 1996
Reprinted 1996

Printed in the United Kingdom at the University Press, Cambridge

A catalogue record for this book is available from the British Library

ISBN 0 521 42207 8 paperback

Designed and produced by Gecko Ltd, Bicester, Oxon

This book is one of a series produced to support
individual modules within the Cambridge Modular
Sciences scheme. Teachers should note that written
examinations will be set on the content of each module
as defined in the syllabus. This book is the authors'
interpretation of the module.

Front cover photograph: A reaction in progress; Erich Schrempp/
Science Photo Library

Contents

Acknowledgements

1, NASA/Science Photo Library; 2, 3, 17, 39*t*, 40*t*, 52, 54, 84, 93, 94, Andrew Lambert; 4, 7, 15, 39*b*, 40*b*, 41 *(main pic)*, Michael Brooke; 6, Tim Fisher/Life File; 25, Mr Ben Mills; 41 *(inset)*, Tick Ahearn; 55, 89, La Belle Aurore; 59; Oxford Molecular Biophysics Laboratory/Science Photo Library; 71, Budd Titlow/f/Stop Pictures; 83, Wildlife Matters; 90*t*, Panda/S Navarrini/Frank Lane Picture Agency; 90*b*, Manfred Kage/Science Photo Library

Chemical energetics

Introduction

For a fleeting instant in astronomical time, the surface of our planet is a ceaseless turmoil of physical and chemical inter-reactions, in startling contrast to the other planets, which plod a sterile course around the Sun. What are the factors that provide the setting for this unique situation, in particular for the provision of the form of chemical phenomena known collectively as 'Life'? Do they arise by mindless chance? Are they under the direction of a benign Creator? What makes it all happen?

One factor is the existence of water. It is found nearly everywhere – the most perfect of all solvents. Its temperature permits it to exist as a liquid, in a small range between 273 and 373 K. Another factor is the presence of the basic atomic building-blocks, particularly carbon, hydrogen, oxygen and nitrogen. Added to these is an atmosphere that maintains and nourishes all the wonderful changes taking place, such as the photosynthesis of plants and the beating of your heart. Within the atmosphere, as we may have realised too late, is the stratospheric ozone layer, which so far has shielded life-forms from the destructive effects of the Sun's ultraviolet (UV) radiation. Humanity now threatens it, along with so many of the systems on which our livelihood and existence depend.

Most important of all is the energy derived from the Sun. It stokes the fires of earthly existence – keeps everything going. In the final analysis the Sun is the only primary source of the energy that drives all the chemical changes occurring within and around us.

It is the purpose of this module to look in some detail at a few of these chemical changes and consider their environmental importance. We shall look at the factors that govern both the *extent* to which reactions occur (how far) and the *rate* at which they occur (how fast). We will use terms like equilibrium, thermochemistry, energetics and kinetics – some of the jargon of chemistry.

● *Figure 1.1* Earth – the great reaction vessel. The most fascinating of its millions of chemical reactions take place on the surface of the planet, many of them inside you!

Chemical reactions and energy change

You should be used to the 'balanced' chemical equation. The one below tells you what happens to a lump of charcoal when it burns, for instance in a barbecue.

$$C(s) + O_2(g) \longrightarrow CO_2(g)$$

In plain English it says that solid carbon reacts with oxygen gas to form carbon dioxide, also a gas.

The equation also tells you about the **stoichiometry** of the reaction, that is, the amounts of each substance involved. It says that one mole of carbon atoms reacts with one mole of oxygen molecules to form one mole of carbon dioxide molecules.

These amounts can be translated into actual masses and volumes. Knowing relative atomic masses, we can say that 12 g of carbon react with 32 g of oxygen to form 44 g of carbon dioxide.

● **Figure 1.2** This 12 g mass of charcoal will react with 32 g of oxygen to produce enough heat to boil the 1 dm³ of water.

This is not a 'So what!' statement – it really affects how we can think about our environment. It helps us to see that every tonne of coal burned produces over three tonnes of carbon dioxide – all destined for our atmosphere, to contribute to global warming. Stoichiometry *is* important!

What the equation above does *not* tell you about is the energy involved. It does not mention the **thermochemistry** of the reaction. It does not tell you how much heat is given out. Chemists have calculated that, in a barbecue, every mole of carbon atoms that burns produces 393 000 J (or 393 kJ) of heat energy. This is more than enough energy to boil a litre (1 dm³) of tap water – a lot of energy from a small lump of charcoal (*figure 1.2*).

Our barbecue reaction is **exothermic** – it is a 'give-out-heat' reaction. This heat is lost to the surroundings (some of it to your kebabs if you are lucky). The other sort of reaction – a 'take-in-heat' reaction or **endothermic** reaction – is useless for cooking, but might be useful in making a cold drink to go with the kebabs.

We can represent the energy changes in the barbecue with an energy diagram (*figure 1.3*). Notice that the energy of what you finish with (carbon dioxide) is less than that of what you started with (carbon and oxygen). Every mole of carbon dioxide formed is accompanied by a *loss* of 393 kJ of heat to the surroundings. There is a change in heat energy between before (C + O₂) and after (CO₂) and the change is negative. In science we represent the term 'change in' with the Greek symbol Δ (delta). Because it refers to heat energy, we call the change 'ΔH'. Because there is less energy in the substance formed (CO₂) than in the reactants (C + O₂), we say that 'ΔH is negative'. The barbecue reaction can now be written as

$$C(s) + O_2(g) \longrightarrow CO_2(g); \qquad \Delta H = -393 \text{ kJ mol}^{-1}$$

The last part is spoken as 'minus 393 kilojoules per mole of carbon dioxide formed'. You need to get used to calling this amount of energy 'the **enthalpy change** of formation of carbon dioxide'.

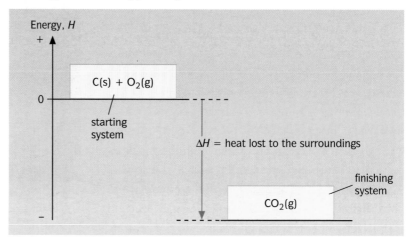

● **Figure 1.3** Energy level diagram for the combustion of carbon dioxide.

Enthalpy

This is a curious and potentially difficult word – one of those words with a meaning that develops the more that you learn. Enthalpy is the total heat content of a system, is given the symbol H, and is measured in joules (J) or kilojoules (kJ).

We live in a world of chemical systems, identifiable sets of substances that can react and change. A system can be simple, like a piece of barbecue charcoal surrounded by oxygen. The system can be more complex, like a piece of barbecued hamburger being digested with the help of oxygen and other chemicals in the body. In both systems, new substances are formed. In both systems, the enthalpy changes too. The change in enthalpy between the old system and the new system is ΔH, provided there is no change in pressure *(box 1A)*. ΔH is negative if the new system has less enthalpy than the old. ΔH is positive if the new system has a greater total heat content than before *(figure 1.4)*.

We can use the term 'enthalpy' in any change that involves the breaking and making of chemical bonds.

When talking about enthalpy, you need to be clear about the kind of change taking place. Two examples, showing the enthalpy change of formation of sulphur dioxide and the enthalpy change of reaction of Alka Seltzer in water, are given in *figures 1.5* and *1.6*. There are many others, as you will find out.

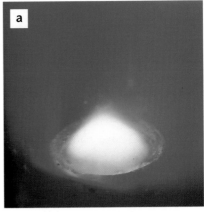

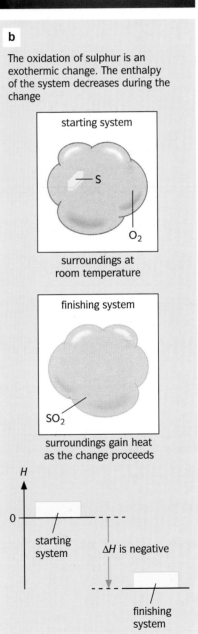

The oxidation of sulphur is an exothermic change. The enthalpy of the system decreases during the change

starting system

S

O_2

surroundings at room temperature

finishing system

SO_2

surroundings gain heat as the change proceeds

H

0

starting system

ΔH is negative

finishing system

● **Figure 1.5 a** Sulphur burning in oxygen. **b** The formation of sulphur dioxide.

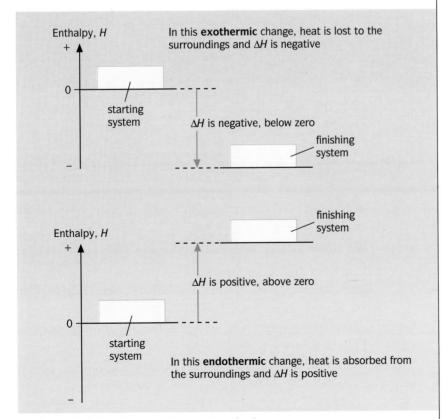

Enthalpy, H

In this **exothermic** change, heat is lost to the surroundings and ΔH is negative

0

starting system

ΔH is negative, below zero

finishing system

Enthalpy, H

finishing system

0

ΔH is positive, above zero

starting system

In this **endothermic** change, heat is absorbed from the surroundings and ΔH is positive

● **Figure 1.4** Exothermic and endothermic changes.

a

b

The reaction of Alka Seltzer in water is an endothermic change. Heat is absorbed from the surroundings, and the enthalpy of the system increases

starting system

water

Alka Seltzer tablet

surroundings at room temperature

finishing system

carbon dioxide

solution

surroundings lose heat to the system as it changes

H

ΔH is positive

0

● *Figure 1.6* The reaction of an Alka Seltzer in water.

Box 1A Enthalpy: heat and work

When you drop a piece of magnesium into a beaker of hydrochloric acid, it reacts. Hydrogen gas and a solution of magnesium chloride are formed.

$$Mg(s) + 2HCl(aq) \longrightarrow H_2(g) + MgCl_2(aq)$$

The hydrogen gas disappears into the atmosphere and the heat generated is lost to the surroundings. The enthalpy change can be estimated by measuring the amount of heat gained by the surroundings.

If, however, you did the reaction in a closed bottle, things would be different. The hydrogen formed cannot escape, so the pressure begins to build up inside the bottle. Assume that the bottle is strong enough to stand the pressure. Part of the energy produced in the reaction is used to do work, i.e. compress the hydrogen. The other part escapes as heat to the surroundings. Any temperature measurements you might make would miss the 'work done' part of the overall enthalpy change *(figure 1.7)*.

To keep life simple at this stage, we only consider reactions that do no work, or very little work, i.e. reactions where the pressure before and after the change is the same.

Magnesium reacting with an acid produces hydrogen. This escapes so the pressure remains the same, i.e. stays constant

Magnesium reacting with an acid produces hydrogen, which cannot escape. The pressure of the system increases during the reaction

● *Figure 1.7* The change in pressure that may occur during a reaction.

Making solutions and investigating energy change

Try the two simple experiments 1 and 2 on page 5. Both are concerned with dissolving a solid in water. In both cases the attractive forces between the ions in the solid are overcome. Energy is needed to do this. In both cases the ions become surrounded by water molecules. Energy is released in the process. Do these changes result in energy being lost from the system (solid + water) as it forms a solution? You can find out for yourself.

Experiment 1

Pour about $20\,cm^3$ of water into a boiling tube. Record its temperature. Add two or three pellets of sodium hydroxide, and stir gently (but constantly) with the thermometer. What happens to the temperature? Try to represent the heat energy change by completing a graph (perhaps like that in *figure 1.4*). Now answer these questions:

- Is heat given out or taken in when sodium hydroxide dissolves in water?
- Is the change exothermic or endothermic?
- Which system contains most energy: (solid + solvent) or (solution)?
- Is ΔH for this change positive or negative? ('ΔH' in this change refers to 'enthalpy change of solution', the amount of heat produced when a mole of solute (NaOH) dissolves in water.)
- How could you represent these changes using an energy diagram?

Experiment 2

Repeat experiment 1, using a spatula-full of ammonium nitrate instead of sodium hydroxide. Then answer these questions:

- Is heat given out or taken in when ammonium nitrate dissolves in water?
- Is the change exothermic or endothermic?
- Which system contains most energy: (solid + solvent) or (solution)?
- Is ΔH for this change positive or negative?
- How could you represent these changes using an energy diagram?

In the first experiment you should notice a considerable rise in temperature. Heat flows out of the system, i.e. the solution and the containing vessel, into the surroundings, i.e. the rest of the Universe! In practice, this means the immediate environment.

When we measure the heat, or energy, that flows out of the system, we use the term **molar enthalpy change of solution**, $\Delta H^{\ominus}_{sol}$. For sodium hydroxide dissolving in water, $\Delta H^{\ominus}_{sol}$ is $-44.5\,kJ\,mol^{-1}$. Let us consider what this really means.

First, we are talking about one mole of sodium hydroxide, NaOH, i.e. 40 g of it. Then we imagine it to dissolve in water until such time that adding extra water makes no difference, i.e. a lot of water. Finally, the symbol $^{\ominus}$ means that it refers to standard conditions, agreed the world over, so that

no confusion arises when scientists communicate with each other. The standard conditions are as follows:

- The temperature of the sodium hydroxide and water is 298 K (25 °C).
- The atmospheric pressure is 101 kPa, i.e. one atmosphere.

The amount of heat given out can be measured by calorimetry with the aid of a balance and a thermometer. It is calculated in joules (J), the SI unit of energy.

A word about units is appropriate here. The joule is a unit of energy. You use energy to do work. You can think of joules in terms of:

- moving a force through a distance (work = force × distance);
- accelerating a mass through a distance (force = mass × acceleration).

When you throw something, you convert chemical energy in your muscles to kinetic energy. To throw this book across the room you'll need about 5 J (a theoretical quantity that we hope you won't want to put into practice). In heat equivalent terms, a joule is the heat required to raise the temperature of 0.2390 g of water by 1 °C.

So that we can compare how different substances are affected by heat, we use a quantity called the specific heat capacity. The specific heat capacity of a substance is the heat energy required to raise the temperature of 1 kg of the substance by 1 °C (1 K).

The following examples might help you to imagine the standard molar enthalpy change of solution of sodium hydroxide in other terms. It is the amount of energy needed to:

- remain alive and asleep for ten minutes;
- cycle at $20\,km\,h^{-1}$ for one minute;
- pull Ranulph Fiennes' sledge across the Antarctic for 25 seconds.

In contrast, when you dissolve one mole of ammonium nitrate in water, considerable heat is taken up. The process is endothermic. This change is utilised in the cold packs used to treat athletic injuries *(figure 1.8)*. When the pack is kneaded, the

● *Figure 1.8* The use of endothermic reactions to treat injuries.

bags of water and ammonium nitrate are broken, and the dissolving produces the cooling effect required. For this process, therefore, the enthalpy of solution is positive, $+25.7 \, \text{kJ} \, \text{mol}^{-1}$.

These molar enthalpy changes of solution represent the sum of the work done on or by the processes of separating the solvent molecules and solute molecules from one another in their pure state and then mixing them to form the solution. The separating and recombining is illustrated in *figure 1.9*.

The processes illustrated are theoretical – we imagine for the sake of convenience that dissolving takes place like this, to help us with the calculations. It is not the actual way in which a solid dissolves in a solvent. However, as you may have observed previously, it is a nice little trick of which scientists are very fond. You will certainly come across it again in this module.

How to measure enthalpy change

You will need to measure amounts of heat energy. You need to use a thermometer to do this, but beware. Thermometers measure how hot things are, not how much heat they contain.

Think about this rather degenerate scene – having a cup of hot black coffee in the bath. A cup of black coffee, about $0.2 \, \text{dm}^3$, at a mouth-scalding temperature of 90°C (363 K), has far less energy in it than a moderately warm bath of $150 \, \text{dm}^3$ at a temperature of 50°C (323 K). Tipping your hot coffee into the bath would make hardly any difference to the amount of heat available – try it!

In all the examples you come across, you will have to calculate a change in enthalpy, ΔH. The calculation on page 7 shows the change in enthalpy

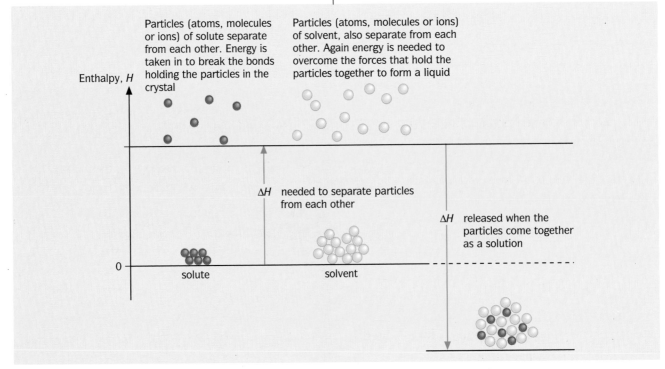

● *Figure 1.9* The enthalpy change of solution.

that occurs when 150 dm³ of water in your bath cools from a comfortable 50 °C to a lukewarm 20 °C. This *change in temperature*, $\Delta T = 30$ °C or 30 K, is what you measure with a thermometer.

The change in enthalpy of the bath, ΔH, is calculated from the equation:
$$\Delta H = \text{mass of water} \times \text{specific heat capacity of water} \times \Delta T$$

Here we have:
Mass of 150 dm³ of water = 150 kg
$$= 150 \times 10^3 \,\text{g}$$
Specific heat capacity of water = 4.18 J g^{-1}K^{-1}

Putting these values in the equation gives
$$\Delta H = 150 \times 10^3 \,\text{g} \times 4.18 \,\text{J g}^{-1}\text{K}^{-1} \times 30 \,\text{K}$$
$$= 18.8 \times 10^6 \,\text{J} = 18\,800 \,\text{kJ}$$

This seems a lot of energy until you work out how many moles of water molecules the bath contains. A mole of water molecules has a mass of only 18 g, so the bath contains $150\,000 \div 18 = 8333$ mol. The change in enthalpy of our bath water is therefore $18\,800 \div 8333 = 2.26$ kJ mol^{-1}, which as enthalpies go is not a lot.

Note that the calculations have ignored the bath itself. If it is a cast-iron bath, it will have stored quite a lot of heat when the hot water went in. This heat would have to be considered when the bath cooled down along with the water. If, however, your bath is made of plastic, the heat stored by the bath would be much less. This is useful to remember when it comes to choosing equipment to do experiments on measuring enthalpy change.

How to measure the enthalpy change of solution $\Delta H^{\ominus}_{sol}$ *of sodium hydroxide*

Method

1 Weigh a polystyrene cup of the kind shown in *figure 1.10*.
2 Weigh 100 g of distilled water into the polystyrene cup. (How could you work out roughly how much to add in advance?)
3 Measure the temperature of the water in the cup *(figure 1.10)*. Keep a check on it until the temperature is steady. Record this temperature.
4 Add a few pellets of solid sodium hydroxide straight from a previously sealed container. (Solid sodium hydroxide absorbs water from the air, so it gets heavier if you leave it standing. **Take care** – it is also very **corrosive**. Wash it off immediately with water if you get it on your skin, and report to your teacher.)
5 Stir the mixture immediately, and start a stopwatch. Keep stirring with the thermometer, and record the temperature every 30 seconds.
6 The temperature will reach a maximum, and then it will start to fall. When it has fallen for five minutes, you can stop taking readings.
7 Weigh the cup + solution to calculate the mass of sodium hydroxide you dissolved.
8 Plot a graph of temperature against time, and work out the maximum temperature the mixture might have reached (see graph in *figure 1.11*).
9 Calculate the amount of heat input to the solution, and calculate the amount of heat given out by the sodium hydroxide and water.
10 Scale the result to tell you how much heat energy would have been released on dissolving one mole (40 g) of sodium hydroxide to make the same strength of solution.

● *Figure 1.10* The apparatus used in school laboratories to measure enthalpy changes.

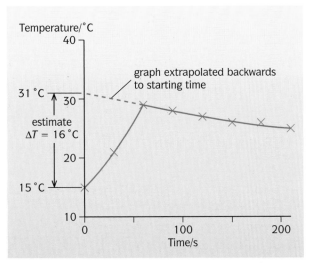

● **Figure 1.11** The results of the example experiment.

A typical set of results

The example below will help you to understand the procedure and calculations:

Mass of polystyrene cup	=	8.00 g
Mass of polystyrene cup + distilled water	=	108.15 g
Mass of distilled water used	=	100.15 g
Mass of cup + water + sodium hydroxide	=	114.35 g
Mass of sodium hydroxide that dissolved	=	6.20 g
Initial temperature of water in the cup	=	16.0 °C

Table showing temperature at fixed times after mixing:

Time/s	0	30	60	90	120	150	180	210
Temperature/°C	15	21	29	28	27	26	26	25

Calculation

Estimated temperature rise caused by 6.2 g NaOH is $\Delta T = 16°C = 16\,K$

$$\Delta H = m \times c \times \Delta T$$

where m = mass of water, c = specific heat capacity of water ($4.18\,Jg^{-1}K^{-1}$), and ΔT = maximum temperature rise. So

$$\Delta H = 100.15\,g \times 4.18\,Jg^{-1}K^{-1} \times 16\,K$$
$$= 6.70\,kJ$$

6.20 g NaOH releases 6.70 kJ energy on dissolving it in water

1 g NaOH would release 6.70 ÷ 6.20 kJ on dissolving in water
so 1 mole of NaOH (40 g) would release 6.70 ÷ 6.20 × 40 kJ

Standard molar enthalpy change

$$\Delta H^{\ominus}_{sol} = \frac{-6.70}{6.20} \times 40\,kJ\,mol^{-1} = -43.2\,kJ\,mol^{-1}$$

Changes of enthalpy that you will meet

Most physical or chemical change is accompanied by a gain or loss of enthalpy, whether it is a snowflake melting or a potato crisp being digested. Here are some of the more common enthalpies described and defined. You need to know and understand them.

Standard enthalpy change of formation $\Delta H^{\ominus}_f(298\,K)$ (figure 1.12)

This is the enthalpy change that occurs when one mole of a compound is formed from its elements at 298 K and at 1 atmosphere (101 kPa) pressure.

Some examples are given below. Note how fractions may need to be introduced on the left-hand side of the equation, to ensure that it represents the formation of one mole of the compound.

$$H_2(g) + \tfrac{1}{2}O_2(g) \longrightarrow H_2O(l);$$
$$\Delta H^{\ominus}_f = -285.9\,kJ\,mol^{-1}$$

$$H_2(g) + O_2(g) \longrightarrow H_2O_2(l);$$
$$\Delta H^{\ominus}_f = -187.6\,kJ\,mol^{-1}$$

$$H_2(g) + 2C(s) \longrightarrow C_2H_2(g);$$
$$\Delta H^{\ominus}_f = +226.8\,kJ\,mol^{-1}$$

$$3H_2(g) + \tfrac{1}{2}O_2(g) + 2C(g) \longrightarrow C_2H_5OH(l);$$
$$\Delta H^{\ominus}_f = -277.1\,kJ\,mol^{-1}$$

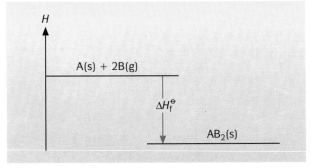

● **Figure 1.12** The standard enthalpy change of formation.

Standard enthalpy change of combustion ΔH°c(298 K) (figure 1.13)

This is the enthalpy change when one mole of an element or compound is burned in excess oxygen under standard conditions.

Here are some examples. Note that fractions may have to be introduced to ensure that the equation represents one mole of compound being burned.

$$C_3H_8(g) + 5O_2(g) \longrightarrow 3CO_2(g) + 4H_2O(l);$$
$$\Delta H^{\ominus}_{c} = -2220 \, kJ \, mol^{-1}$$
$$H_2(g) + \tfrac{1}{2}O_2(g) \longrightarrow H_2O(l);$$
$$\Delta H^{\ominus}_{c} = -285.9 \, kJ \, mol^{-1}$$

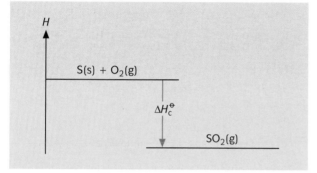

● **Figure 1.13** The standard enthalpy change of combustion.

Standard enthalpy change of hydration ΔH°hyd(298 K) (figure 1.14)

This is the enthalpy change when one mole of ions, existing separately from each other as if the ions were a gas, are surrounded by water molecules to form an 'infinitely dilute solution' under standard conditions.

This type of enthalpy change is a calculated value, one that enables other useful calculations to be made. It is not an enthalpy that can be observed and measured directly, unlike the previous two.

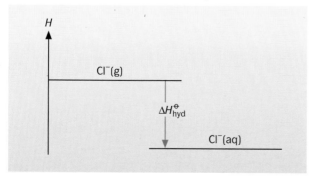

● **Figure 1.14** The standard enthalpy change of hydration.

Standard enthalpy change of solution ΔH°sol(298 K) (figure 1.15)

This is the enthalpy change when one mole of solute is dissolved in a solvent (usually water) so that any further dilution at 298 K and 1 atm pressure brings about no further change in enthalpy. Some examples are:

$$NH_4NO_3(s) \xrightarrow{\text{excess } H_2O(l)} NH_4^+(aq) + NO_3^-(aq);$$
$$\Delta H^{\ominus}_{sol} = +25.7 \, kJ \, mol^{-1}$$
$$KOH(s) \xrightarrow{\text{excess } H_2O(l)} K^+(aq) + OH^-(aq);$$
$$\Delta H^{\ominus}_{sol} = -55.4 \, kJ \, mol^{-1}$$

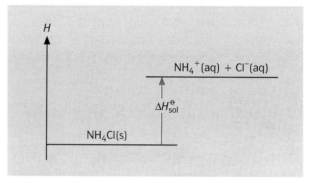

● **Figure 1.15** The standard enthalpy change of solution.

Standard enthalpy change of neutralisation ΔH°n(298 K) (figure 1.16)

This is the enthalpy change when one mole of water molecules are formed when an acid reacts with an alkali at 298 K and 1 atm pressure. For example:

$$\tfrac{1}{2}H_2SO_4(aq) + NaOH(aq)$$
$$\longrightarrow H_2O(l) + \tfrac{1}{2}Na_2SO_4(aq)$$

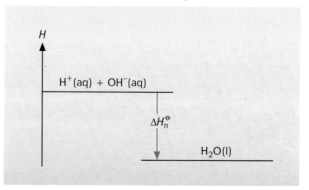

● **Figure 1.16** The standard enthalpy change of neutralisation.

There is really only one reaction involved, i.e. the neutralisation of a mole of positive hydrogen ions from an acid with a mole of negative hydroxide ions from an alkali:

$$H^+(aq) + OH^-(aq) \longrightarrow H_2O(l);$$
$$\Delta H^{\ominus}_n = -57.1 \, kJ \, mol^{-1}$$

Thus any acid–base reaction in which a mole of water molecules is formed is an exothermic reaction releasing 57.1 kJ of heat energy.

SAQ 1.1

Predict the enthalpy change that could be measured when a mole of sulphuric acid molecules in a dilute solution is neutralised by a solution of sodium hydroxide at 298 K and normal pressure.

Standard enthalpy change of atomisation $\Delta H^{\ominus}_{at}$(298 K) (figure 1.17)

This is the enthalpy change required to produce one mole of gaseous atoms from the element at 298 K and 1 atm pressure.

A monatomic gas is a gas made of individual atoms, quite a rare occurrence. The noble gases, such as argon and krypton, are monatomic. However, most gases that are also elements are diatomic, i.e. consist of molecules that are them-selves made of two identical atoms bonded together.

At 298 K and 1 atm pressure, oxygen consists of diatomic molecules, O_2. The enthalpy change of atomisation is the energy required to break one mole of the covalent chemical bonds within the molecules and to separate them as far apart as possible:

$$\tfrac{1}{2}O_2(g) \longrightarrow O(g); \qquad \Delta H^{\ominus}_{at} = +249.2 \, kJ \, mol^{-1}$$

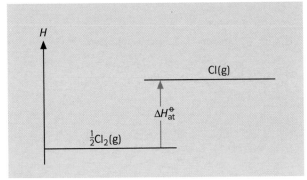

● **Figure 1.17** The standard enthalpy change of atomisation.

Wherever you come across half moles in equations, try to work out the logic for it. It is usually because we are particularly interested in having one mole of atoms or ions elsewhere in the equation.

SAQ 1.2

Figures 1.18–1.22 illustrate each of the six standard enthalpy changes that we have described above (one diagram can represent two of the six). They are not in the same order. Try to match each standard enthalpy change with the appropriate drawing. Then try to write equations that could represent each of the drawings. (In some cases there will only be one correct answer – in others there may be several.)

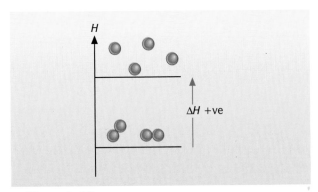

● *Figure 1.18*

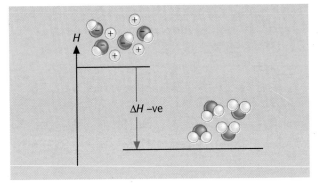

● *Figure 1.19*

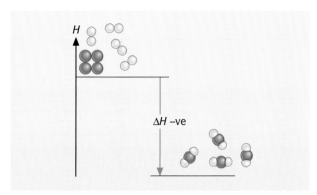

● *Figure 1.20*

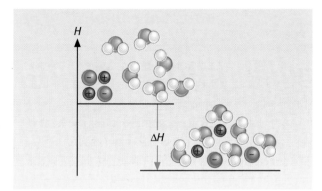

● *Figure 1.21*

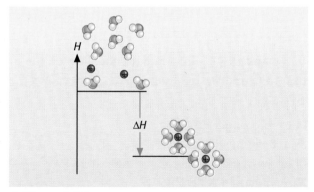

● *Figure 1.22*

A more general enthalpy change

The **enthalpy change of reaction** is the heat energy taken in or given out during a specified reaction, carried out at constant pressure; it is a more general quantity than the enthalpy changes we have looked at so far, in that the quantities of reactants or products are not specified, and the temperature does not have to be 298 K.

For example, consider the reaction when 2 mol of oxygen molecules are atomised to form 4 mol of oxygen atoms:

$$2O_2(g) \longrightarrow 4O(g)$$

If we were to measure the enthalpy change of reaction at 298 K and 1 atm pressure (let's stick to 298 K for now), we should get a value of around $+996.8 \, \text{kJ mol}^{-1}$. Note that this is *not* the standard enthalpy change of atomisation for oxygen, because we are looking at the formation of 4 mol, not 1 mol, of oxygen atoms. The enthalpy change of reaction we measured is, in fact, four times the standard enthalpy change of atomisation of oxygen.

Hess's law

Consider another example of the enthalpy change of reaction. When you switch on the gas supply to a Bunsen burner and ignite the gas, this reaction occurs:

$$CH_4(g) + 2O_2(g) \longrightarrow CO_2(g) + 2H_2O(g);$$
enthalpy change of reaction,
$$\Delta H_1 = -802 \, \text{kJ mol}^{-1} \quad (1.1)$$

This is *not* the standard enthalpy change of combustion of methane, because the water produced is in the form of steam (it is in the gaseous phase because the temperature at which this reaction occurs is higher than 373 K). To measure the standard enthalpy change of combustion of methane, we have to add in the enthalpy change of reaction for 2 mol steam condensing to 2 mol water:

$$2H_2O(g) \longrightarrow 2H_2O(l); \quad \Delta H_2 = -88 \, \text{kJ mol}^{-1}$$
$$(1.2)$$

We must add together *reactions 1.1* and *1.2* to get the overall reaction we want:

$$CH_4(g) + 2O_2(g) \longrightarrow CO_2(g) + 2H_2O(l)$$
$$(1.3)$$

We can represent the addition of these reactions by a diagram; *figures 1.23* and *1.24* show two

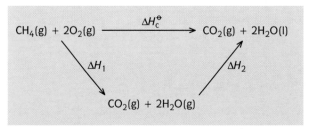

● *Figure 1.23* A Hess's law triangle for the combustion of methane.

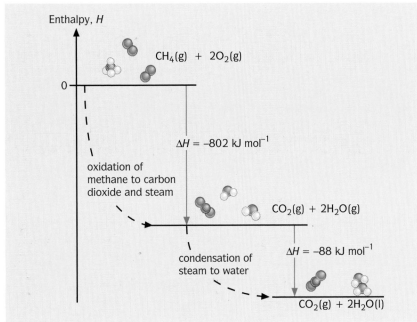

● **Figure 1.24** The enthalpy changes involved in the combustion of methane.

different ways of doing this. Note that the diagrams show that there are two different routes for achieving *reaction 1.3*; we call these routes **reaction pathways**. Note also that each pathway starts with the same reactants under the same conditions, and finishes with the same products under the same conditions, even though different compounds may be formed under different conditions in the middle of the pathway.

So we can say that the standard enthalpy change of combustion of methane, $\Delta H^{\ominus}_{c}$, is given by:

$$\Delta H_c = \Delta H_1 + \Delta H_2$$
$$= -802 + (-88)\,\mathrm{kJ\,mol^{-1}}$$
$$= -890\,\mathrm{kJ\,mol^{-1}}$$

This is an example of **Hess's law**:

The enthalpy change in a reaction is the same regardless of the pathway by which the reaction occurs, provided that the initial and final conditions are the same.

Figure 1.23 is often called a **Hess's law triangle**.

Hess's law applied

Hess's law helps us to make predictions about the values of certain enthalpy changes if experimental data are not available.

It is possible to estimate by experiment the enthalpy change in the combustion of ethanol. By burning ethanol in oxygen, and using the heat (hopefully all of it) to raise the temperature of a metal can containing water, a value can be obtained. The method used is explained below.

Finding the enthalpy change of combustion of ethanol

The equipment in *figure 1.25* can be used to find a rough value for any liquid fuel that can be burned safely.

If we assume that all the heat of the flame is transferred to the water, then the heat produced by a weighed amount of ethanol burning is given as

heat produced = mass of water × specific heat of water × temperature rise
$$= m \times c \times \Delta T$$

In practice this equipment does not allow all the heat to be transferred to the water. Heat is also given out:

■ to the copper can itself;
■ to heating air that misses the can;
■ by convection to air above the water;
■ by radiation generally.

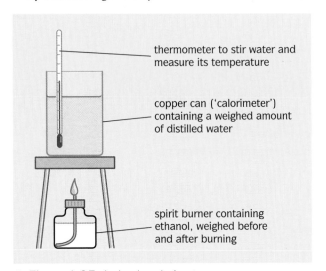

● **Figure 1.25** A simple calorimeter.

The apparatus in *figure 1.26* helps to overcome these sources of error. The apparatus is isolated from the outside by insulation, so much less heat is given out to the surroundings, and more of the air heated is used to heat the can. The can is filled with water, so convection to the air is reduced.

The calculations in *box 1C* will help you to understand more about the method used.

Calculating enthalpy changes of formation using Hess's law

Suppose you need to find the enthalpy change of formation of ethane (*not* the enthalpy change of combustion):

$$2C(s) + 3H_2(g) \longrightarrow C_2H_6(g); \quad \Delta H_f = ? \quad (1.4)$$

This reaction cannot be carried out in the laboratory. However, knowing the standard enthalpy

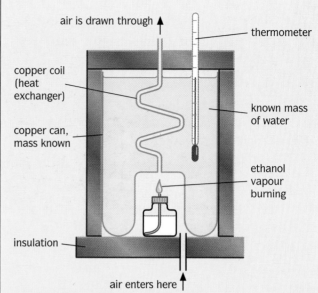

The apparatus should also have a stirrer in the water. This has been left out to simplify the diagram

● *Figure 1.26* A more advanced calorimeter.

Box 1C

Using the apparatus in *figure 1.25*:

Mass of water in the can	= 250 g
Rise in temperature of water	= 10 K
Specific heat of water	= 4.2 J g^{-1}K^{-1}
Mass of ethanol burned	= 0.53 g
Mass of 1 mol ethanol	= 46 g

Calculation for *figure 1.25*

Heat gained by water $= m \times c \times \Delta T$
$$= 250\,g \times 4.2\,J\,g^{-1}K^{-1} \times 10\,K$$
$$= 10\,500\,J$$
$$= 10.5\,kJ$$

Heat produced by 0.53 g ethanol = 10.5 kJ
    (assuming no heat given out in the process)

Heat produced by 1 g ethanol $= \dfrac{10.5\,kJ}{0.53}$

Heat produced by 1 mol ethanol $= \dfrac{46 \times 10.5\,kJ}{0.53}$
$$= 911\,kJ$$

Using the apparatus in *figure 1.26*:

Mass of water in calorimeter	= 300 g
Rise in temperature of water	= 10 K
Specific heat of water	= 4.2 J g^{-1}K^{-1}
Mass of copper apparatus	= 220 g
Specific heat of copper	= 0.38 J g^{-1}K^{-1}
Mass of ethanol burned	= 0.47 g

Calculation for *figure 1.26*

Heat taken in by water $= m \times c \times \Delta T$
$$= 300\,g \times 4.2\,J\,g^{-1}K^{-1} \times 10\,K$$
$$= 12\,600\,J$$

Heat taken in by apparatus $= m \times c \times \Delta T$
$$= 220\,g \times 0.38\,J\,g^{-1}K^{-1}$$
$$\times 10\,K$$
$$= 836\,J$$

Total heat taken in = 12 600 J + 836 J
$$= 13\,436\,J = 13.4\,kJ \text{ (to 3 sig figs)}$$

Heat produced by 0.47 g ethanol = 13.4 kJ
    (assuming no heat given out in the process)

Heat produced by 1 mol ethanol $= \dfrac{46 \times 13.4\,kJ}{0.47}$
$$= 1311\,kJ$$

Hence, enthalpy change of combustion of ethanol
$$= -1311\,kJ\,mol^{-1}$$

The accepted answer for the enthalpy change of combustion of ethanol, $\Delta H^{\ominus}_c$, is actually $-1370\,kJ\,mol^{-1}$. The experimental value is still too low, but some heat losses are inevitable, particularly because some of the air that is heated still passes by the can.

changes for the combustion of carbon, hydrogen and ethane enables us to make the required calculation:

$$C_2H_6(g) + \tfrac{7}{2}O_2(g) \longrightarrow 2CO_2(g) + 3H_2O(l);$$
$$\Delta H^{\oplus}_c = -1560\,kJ\,mol^{-1} \quad (1.5)$$

$$C(s) + O_2(g) \longrightarrow CO_2(g);$$
$$\Delta H^{\oplus}_c = -393\,kJ\,mol^{-1} \quad (1.6)$$

$$H_2(g) + \tfrac{1}{2}O_2(g) \longrightarrow H_2O(l);$$
$$\Delta H^{\oplus}_c = -286\,kJ\,mol^{-1} \quad (1.7)$$

We need to manipulate these three equations so that when they are added together they create the desired *reaction 1.4*. This can be achieved in two ways.

■ Method 1

First reverse *reaction 1.5*. This puts ethane on the side of the equation you want it to be, i.e. being formed. Note that the sign of ΔH must also be changed. We now have

$$2CO_2(g) + 3H_2O(l) \longrightarrow C_2H_6(g) + \tfrac{7}{2}O_2(g);$$
$$\Delta H = +1560\,kJ\,mol^{-1} \quad (1.8)$$

Now look at the numbers of molecules of carbon dioxide and water making up ethane, i.e. 2 and 3 respectively. Multiply *reaction 1.6* by 2

and *reaction 1.7* by 3 and add them together with *reaction 1.8*:

$$2C(s) + 2O_2(g) \longrightarrow 2CO_2(g);$$
$$\Delta H_c = -786\,kJ\,mol^{-1} \quad (1.9)$$

$$3H_2(g) + \tfrac{3}{2}O_2(g) \longrightarrow 3H_2O(l);$$
$$\Delta H_c = -858\,kJ\,mol^{-1} \quad (1.10)$$

$$2CO_2(g) + 3H_2O(l) \longrightarrow C_2H_6(g) + \tfrac{7}{2}O_2(g);$$
$$\Delta H = +1560\,kJ\,mol^{-1} \quad (1.8)$$

$$\overline{}$$

$$2C(s) + 3H_2(g) \longrightarrow C_2H_6(g);$$
$$\Delta H_f = -84\,kJ\,mol^{-1}$$

■ Method 2

The enthalpy change of formation of ethane can also be found by constructing a Hess's law triangle (*figure 1.27*).

Applying Hess's law:

  enthalpy change by steps 1 and 4
  = enthalpy change by steps 2 and 3

So the enthalpy change of formation of ethane (step 1), ΔH_f, is given by:

$$\Delta H_f = \text{step 2} + \text{step 3} - \text{step 4}$$
$$= (-786) + (-858)$$
$$\quad - (-1560)\,kJ\,mol^{-1}$$
$$= -84\,kJ\,mol^{-1}$$

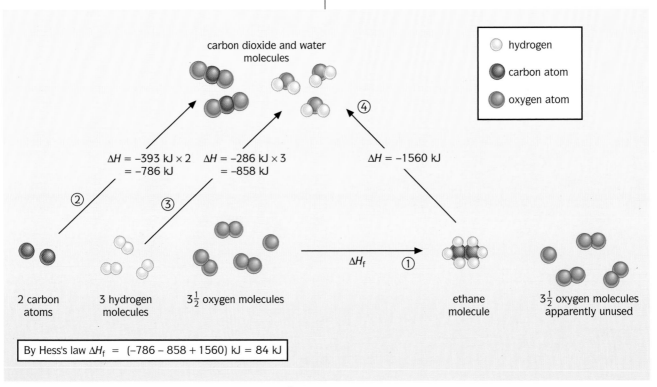

$\Delta H = -393\,kJ \times 2$ $\Delta H = -286\,kJ \times 3$ $\Delta H = -1560\,kJ$
$= -786\,kJ$ $= -858\,kJ$

carbon dioxide and water molecules

○ hydrogen
● carbon atom
● oxygen atom

2 carbon atoms 3 hydrogen molecules $3\tfrac{1}{2}$ oxygen molecules ΔH_f ethane molecule $3\tfrac{1}{2}$ oxygen molecules apparently unused

By Hess's law $\Delta H_f = (-786 - 858 + 1560)\,kJ = 84\,kJ$

● **Figure 1.27** Hess's law applied to the combustion of ethane.

Reactions *1.8*, *1.9* and *1.10* suggest a way for making ethane from carbon and hydrogen, by way of their oxides. This is not the case, but we may imagine it to be so. Then by applying Hess's law we can calculate that the heat of formation of ethane, $\Delta H_f = (-786 - 856 + 1560)\,\text{kJ}\,\text{mol}^{-1} = -84\,\text{kJ}\,\text{mol}^{-1}$.

Lattice energy

A lattice is a repeating geometrical pattern – like the panes of glass in lattice windows *(figure 1.28)*.

Many solids exist as ionic lattices, a repeating pattern in three dimensions. The lattice for sodium chloride is shown in *figure 1.29*.

The **lattice energy** $\Delta H^{\ominus}_{latt}$ (298 K) is the enthalpy change when a mole of an ionic compound is formed from its separate ions in the gaseous state *(figure 1.30)*. For example:

$$Na^+(g) + Cl^-(g) \longrightarrow Na^+Cl^-(s);$$
$$\Delta H^{\ominus}_{latt} = -771\,\text{kJ}\,\text{mol}^{-1}$$

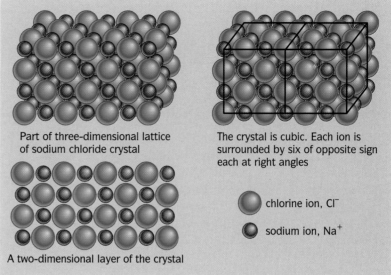

Part of three-dimensional lattice of sodium chloride crystal

The crystal is cubic. Each ion is surrounded by six of opposite sign each at right angles

chlorine ion, Cl⁻

sodium ion, Na⁺

A two-dimensional layer of the crystal

● *Figure 1.29* The lattice for sodium chloride.

$$Mg^{2+}(g) + 2F^-(g) \longrightarrow Mg^{2+}(F^-)_2(s);$$
$$\Delta H^{\ominus}_{latt} = -2883\,\text{kJ}\,\text{mol}^{-1}$$
$$Ca^{2+}(g) + O^{2-}(g) \longrightarrow Ca^{2+}O^{2-}(s);$$
$$\Delta H^{\ominus}_{latt} = -3523\,\text{kJ}\,\text{mol}^{-1}$$

It is not always easy to answer the question 'A mole of what?' when talking about ionic compounds. For example, a mole of calcium chloride, $CaCl_2$, consists of one mole of calcium ions, Ca^{2+}, combined with two moles of chlorine ions, $2Cl^-$. Writing formulae and equations helps to clarify the situation.

● *Figure 1.28* Two kinds of lattice.

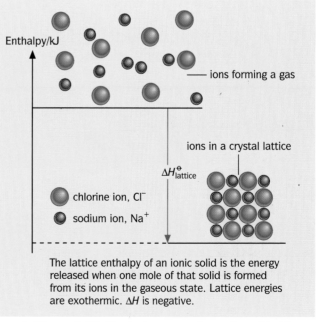

Enthalpy/kJ

ions forming a gas

ions in a crystal lattice

$\Delta H^{\ominus}_{lattice}$

chlorine ion, Cl⁻

sodium ion, Na⁺

The lattice enthalpy of an ionic solid is the energy released when one mole of that solid is formed from its ions in the gaseous state. Lattice energies are exothermic. ΔH is negative.

● *Figure 1.30* The lattice energy for sodium chloride.

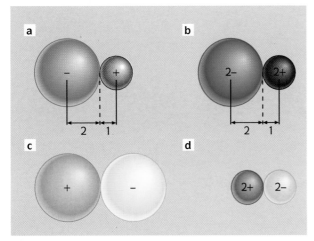

● **Figure 1.31** Measuring bond strengths.

Nobody actually creates a situation like a gas of ions at 298 K that condenses to form the solid. Lattice energy refers to a hypothetical change. It is simply a convenient notion, a useful one to imagine. Not surprisingly, this hypothetical change is exothermic. A high lattice energy is a sign of strong bonding in the solid. This bonding depends upon a number of factors, all affecting the strength of attraction between the ions that make up the crystal:

■ the charges on the constituent ions – the higher the charge, the stronger the attraction;
■ the sizes of the ions – the smaller the ion, the stronger the attraction.

SAQ 1.3

Figure 1.31 shows pairs of ions of different charge and size. Rank these ion pairs in order of increasing bond strength.

The Born–Haber cycle

A knowledge of lattice enthalpy is critical for deciding whether an ionic solid is likely to result from the constituent elements in their standard state. To make this decision, we use the Born–Haber cycle. This uses the same sort of rationale as Hess's law, that the overall enthalpy change of a process will be the sum of the separate enthalpy changes of the separate steps, whatever pathway is taken. The Born–Haber cycle for the lattice enthalpy of a salt is set out in *figure 1.32*.

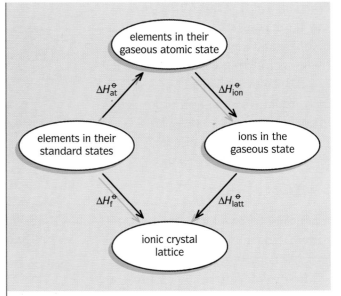

● **Figure 1.32** The Born–Haber cycle for the lattice energy of a salt.

Figure 1.33 provides the requisite values and calculation for the lattice energy of sodium chloride. This turns out to be a large quantity commensurate with high stability – as we might have expected – we need it on our fish and chips!

Figure 1.34 shows in more detail an energy pathway for the formation of sodium chloride from its elements. *This is not a reaction mechanism.* Gaseous ions of sodium are not formed when sodium and chlorine react together

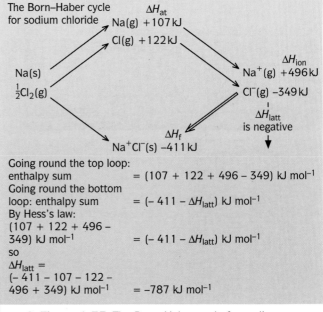

The Born–Haber cycle for sodium chloride

ΔH_{at} Na(g) +107 kJ
Cl(g) +122 kJ

Na(s)
$\frac{1}{2}Cl_2(g)$

ΔH_{ion}
Na$^+$(g) +496 kJ
Cl$^-$(g) −349 kJ

ΔH_{latt} is negative

ΔH_f
Na$^+$Cl$^-$(s) −411 kJ

Going round the top loop: enthalpy sum = (107 + 122 + 496 − 349) kJ mol^{-1}
Going round the bottom loop: enthalpy sum = (− 411 − ΔH_{latt}) kJ mol^{-1}
By Hess's law:
(107 + 122 + 496 − 349) kJ mol^{-1} = (− 411 − ΔH_{latt}) kJ mol^{-1}
so
ΔH_{latt} = (− 411 − 107 − 122 − 496 + 349) kJ mol^{-1} = −787 kJ mol^{-1}

● **Figure 1.33** The Born–Haber cycle for sodium chloride.

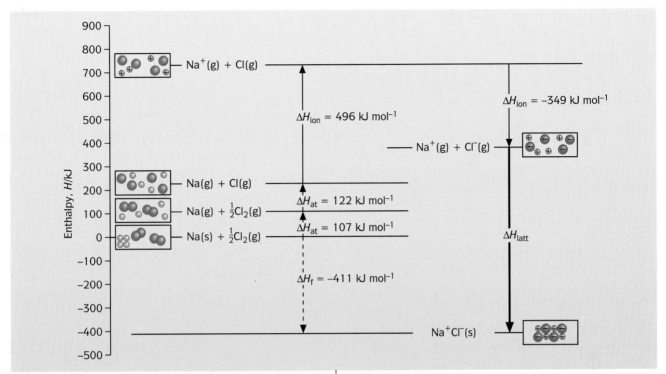

● *Figure 1.34* An energy diagram for the formation of sodium chloride.

as shown in the photograph in *figure 1.35*. It is simply an accounting method for reaction enthalpies.

The diagram includes ionisation energies and enthalpy changes of electron affinity. You have met

● *Figure 1.35* Sodium burning in chlorine gas.

ionisation energy before, but you may need reminding. The first ionisation energy of an element, $\Delta H^{\ominus}_{ion}$, is the energy needed to remove one mole of electrons from one mole of gaseous atoms.

$$X(g) \longrightarrow X^+(g) + e^-$$

It is always an endothermic change, so ΔH is positive.

Enthalpy change of electron affinity, $\Delta H^{\ominus}_e$, is similar. However, the enthalpy change is negative – the process is exothermic. The first electron affinity again refers to a mole of atoms of an element in the gaseous state, but this time each atom gains a single negative charge (by accepting an electron). The enthalpy change of electron affinity, $\Delta H^{\ominus}_e$, is defined as the energy released when a mole of atoms of an element in the gaseous state acquires a mole of electrons to become a mole of ions each with a single negative charge.

Bond energies from Hess's law

During any chemical change, chemical bonds are broken, and chemical bonds are remade. In other words, the forces that hold atoms together in molecules, ions together in crystal lattices, or atoms within giant structures are overcome and then allowed to come into play again in a completely different arrangement.

To overcome a force, energy is needed. This can vary a great deal. In the liquid state, water molecules are connected by hydrogen bonds. When water evaporates, the bonds are broken. The energy needed to do this is relatively low ($40.7\,kJ\,mol^{-1}$). The energy needed to separate two hydrogen atoms in a mole of hydrogen molecules, H_2, is much larger ($436\,kJ\,mol^{-1}$).

Bond energy always refers to bonds within molecules of gases. It is defined as the amount of energy needed to break one mole of identical covalent bonds between atoms within the molecules. Thus the bond energy of iodine is the energy required to overcome the forces holding a mole of iodine molecules together so that a gas of iodine atoms is formed.

Bond energies range from about $50\,kJ\,mol^{-1}$ to $900\,kJ\,mol^{-1}$, reflecting the differing nature of the various bonds and the structures of the atoms involved. Bond energies can be useful tools to the chemist, and some selected bond energies are given in *table 1.1*. Note that the bond energies between atoms of the same kind can vary. Look for patterns, for instance the change in bond strengths in going from single to double to triple bonds. Bear in mind that the molecule itself can determine to some degree the strength of the bond, for example C–H in methane compared to C–H in ethyne. Some general values for

Diatomic molecules of gases/vapours					
H–H	436	(in H_2)	Cl–Cl	244	(in Cl_2)
F–F	158	(in F_2)	I–I	151	(in I_2)
Br–Br	193	(in Br_2)	O=O	496	(in O_2)
P≡P	488	(in P_2)	H–Cl	431	(in HCl)
N≡N	945	(in N_2)	H–I	299	(in HI)
H–Br	366	(in HBr)			

Polyatomic molecules (more than two atoms per molecule)					
C–C	350		H–N	390	(in NH_3)
C=C	610		N–N	160	(in N_2H_4)
C≡C	840		N=N	410	
C∷C	520	(in benzene)	H–O	460	
C–H	410		O–O	150	
C–Cl	340		P–P	201	(in P_4)
C–Br	280		Si–H	320	
C–I	240		Si–Cl	359	
C–O	360		Si–O	444	
C=O	803	(in CO_2)	Si–Si	222	
C=O	740		S–Cl	250	
S–H	347		S–S	264	

● *Table 1.1* Some covalent bond energies ($kJ\,mol^{-1}$)

certain bonds are given as good working bond energies, irrespective of the molecules in which they occur. When in doubt, use these.

Bond energies can be calculated from spectroscopic data. This shows that bond energies are not just a function of atoms involved, but also the situation in which they are found. For example, the energy needed to separate one atom of hydrogen from a molecule of water is less than that required to separate the second:

$$H-O-H(g) \longrightarrow H(g) + O-H(g); \qquad \Delta H = +430\,kJ\,mol^{-1}$$
$$O-H(g) \longrightarrow H(g) + O(g); \qquad \Delta H = +498\,kJ\,mol^{-1}$$

We therefore refer to *average* bond energies. For the O–H bond the value of $(430 + 498) \div 2 = 464\,kJ\,mol^{-1}$ produces a figure close to the one quoted above.

Bond energies can be estimated from thermochemical data by applying Hess's Law. If you can set up a system that includes a mole of bonds being formed or being broken, and if you can supply all the rest of the data for the changes you imagine, then you can estimate the bond energy – regardless of whether the system actually occurs in practice or not. An example is given in *figure 1.36*.

You need to imagine this situation: four individual atoms of hydrogen and one of carbon come together to form a methane molecule, CH_4. In so doing four carbon–hydrogen covalent bonds, C–H, are formed *(figure 1.36)*.

The equation for the reaction would be

$$C(g) + 4H(g) \longrightarrow CH_4(g); \qquad \Delta H_1 = ?\,kJ\,mol^{-1} \qquad (1.11)$$

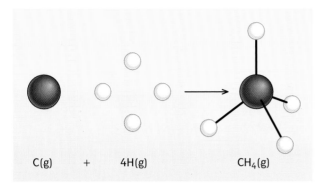

● **Figure 1.36** The formation of methane.

We can build up the left-hand side of the equation using other reactions we can visualise, and for which we have data. It is best to start from the reaction of solid carbon with gaseous hydrogen to form methane. It bridges the elements with the product, methane, and we have data for the reaction (the enthalpy of formation of methane):

$$C(s) + 2H_2(g) \longrightarrow CH_4(g);$$
$$\Delta H_f = -74.8 \, kJ \, mol^{-1} \qquad (1.12)$$

We then build up to the left-hand side of *reaction 1.11*, with the intention of atomising each element:

$$C(s) \longrightarrow C(g);$$
$$\Delta H_f = 715 \, kJ \, mol^{-1} \qquad (1.13)$$
$$2H_2(g) \longrightarrow 4H(g);$$
$$\Delta H_f = 4 \times 218 \, kJ \, mol^{-1} \qquad (1.14)$$

We can then create a cycle and apply Hess's law (*figure 1.37*).

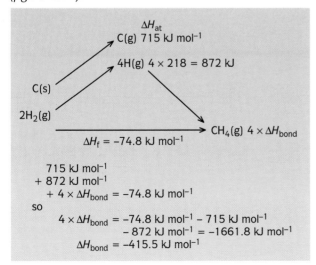

● **Figure 1.37** Hess's law applied to the formation of methane.

SUMMARY

■ Many chemical reactions are accompanied by energy changes, principally in the form of heat energy.

■ Changes in the energy of reacting chemicals are known as *enthalpy changes* (ΔH). *Exothermic* enthalpy changes have negative ΔH values, where heat energy is transferred away from the reacting chemicals. *Endothermic* enthalpy changes have positive ΔH values, where heat energy is transferred into the reacting chemicals.

■ In experiments that measure changes in temperature during a reaction, enthalpy change = $mc\Delta T$, where m is the mass of the apparatus (often a water bath), c is the specific heat capacity of the apparatus and ΔT is the measured temperature change.

■ Standard conditions for enthalpy changes are a pressure of 101 kPa and a temperature of 298 K. Solutions must be at a concentration of 1 mol dm^{-3}. Reactants and products must be in specified physical states, depending on the type of enthalpy change under consideration.

■ *Bond energy* is a measure of the energy required to break a bond.

■ The *lattice energy* is a measure of the 'strength' of an ionic lattice; it is the enthalpy change when one mole of an ionic compound is formed from its separate ions in the gaseous state.

■ Lattice energy is greater for smaller ions and for ions with greater charge on them.

■ Hess's law states that 'the total enthalpy change for a chemical reaction is independent of the route by which the reaction takes place'. This principle can be used to calculate enthalpy changes for reactions that cannot be carried out directly in an experiment.

Questions

1 The specific heat capacity of water is often quoted as $4.18\,J\,g^{-1}\,K^{-1}$. Explain what this means in words by considering what 4.18 joules of heat energy can actually do to a sample of water.

How many joules of heat energy can raise the temperature of 1 g of water by 1°C? Explain your answer.

2 Which of the following are **endothermic** changes?
   a the formation of S_2 molecules from S_8 molecules;
   b the absorption of ultraviolet radiation by ozone molecules;
   c the rusting of iron;
   d the formation of iodine crystals when iodine vapour sublimes;
   e the dissociation of ammonium chloride crystals into hydrogen chloride gas and ammonia gas.

3 In which of these changes is ΔH **negative**?
   a the formation of diamond from graphite;
   b the production of a direct current from a dry cell;
   c the electrolysis of an aqueous copper sulphate solution;
   d the absorption of light energy by silver halides;
   e the reaction of sulphur trioxide with water.

4 Examine the Born–Haber cycle in *figure 1.38*.
   a ΔH_4 is the enthalpy change of solution of magnesium chloride. What should be written where each question mark is placed?
   b What kind of enthalpy change is ΔH_1?
   c What kind of enthalpy change is ΔH_2?
   d $\Delta H_1 = -2489\,kJ\,mol^{-1}$, $\Delta H_2 = -1891\,kJ\,mol^{-1}$ and $\Delta H_3 = -381\,kJ\,mol^{-1}$. Calculate the enthalpy change of solution of magnesium chloride.
   e What would you observe if magnesium chloride was stirred up in a beaker of distilled water?

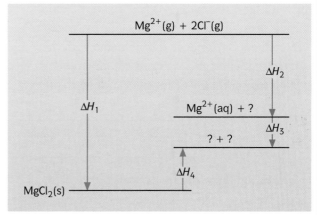

● *Figure 1.38*

5 Find the relationship between lattice enthalpy, enthalpy of hydration and enthalpy of solution for an ionic solid. Draw a Born–Haber cycle to illustrate this with reference to potassium bromide.

Chapter two

Electrochemistry

By the end of this chapter you should be able to:

1 understand the term *redox*;

2 describe and explain redox processes in terms of both electron transfer and changes in oxidation number;

3 define and use the terms *standard electrode potential* and *standard cell potential*;

4 describe and understand the function of the standard hydrogen electrode;

5 describe methods used to measure the standard electrode potentials of **a** atoms in contact with an aqueous solution of their ions and **b** ions of the same element present in different oxidation states;

6 calculate a standard cell potential by combining two standard electrode potentials;

7 use standard cell potentials **a** to explain and predict the direction of electron flow from a simple cell and **b** to predict whether a reaction might occur;

8 construct redox equations using the relevant half-equations;

9 understand how the electrode potential varies with the concentration of the aqueous ion.

Redox reviewed and renewed

Reduction and oxidation are old chemical ideas – useful ones – which have changed and developed over the years. Oxidation once had a simple description – the process that occurs when a substance combines with oxygen. The burning of sulphur or the heating of copper in oxygen are simple examples:

$$S(s) \ + \ O_2(g) \longrightarrow SO_2(g)$$
— oxidised —

$$2Cu(s) \ + \ O_2(g) \longrightarrow 2CuO(s)$$
— oxidised —

In each case the element combines with oxygen to become an oxide – the idea of oxidation is simple and obvious.

Reduction is the chemical opposite of oxidation. Copper(II) oxide can have its oxygen removed by

hot hydrogen so that copper metal is formed. In the process the hydrogen is itself oxidised:

— reduced —
$$CuO(s) + H_2(g) \xrightarrow{\text{heat}} Cu(s) + H_2O(g)$$
— oxidised —

Reduction goes hand-in-hand with oxidation – hence the term 'redox'.

The substance causing the reduction is called the reducing agent.

SAQ 2.1

Look at the redox reaction between lead(II) oxide and carbon monoxide:

$$PbO(s) + CO(g) \xrightarrow{\text{heat}} Pb(s) + CO_2(g)$$

What substance is reduced? What substance is oxidised? What is the reducing agent? What is the oxidising agent?

The whole idea of oxidation and reduction is very useful in the metals industry, whether it involves extracting metals from ores (reduction) or investigating corrosion (oxidation). Sometimes, however, metal extraction and corrosion do not involve oxygen at all. For example, metallic copper can be extracted from a solution of copper chloride using a more reactive metal such as magnesium. The copper(II) ions are reduced to copper atoms by the magnesium. The reducing agent (magnesium) corrodes and oxidises in the process:

— oxidised —
$$CuCl_2(aq) + Mg(s) \longrightarrow Cu(s) \ + \ MgCl_2(aq)$$
— reduced —

Another example is shown in *figure 2.1*.

In an atmosphere of chlorine, iron corrodes, forming a rust-like material, iron(III) chloride:

$$2Fe(s) + 3Cl_2(g) \longrightarrow 2FeCl_3(s)$$

It is quite neat to think of this as another form of oxidation, but without oxygen. A metal has corroded – combined with a reactive gas to become a compound.

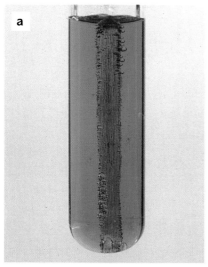

● **Figure 2.1**

a Fresh magnesium placed in copper sulphate solution.

b The result of magnesium reacting with copper sulphate.

SAQ 2.2

For the reaction between chlorine and iron: What has been oxidised when iron reacts with chlorine? What is the oxidising agent? What has been reduced in the process?

Reduction and oxidation occur during electrolysis

In the example in *figure 2.2*, the negative electrode (made of carbon) becomes coated with copper metal – an example of reduction. At the same time the positive electrode (made of copper) corrodes – an example of oxidation. The flow of electrons through the solution is the key to it all *(figure 2.3)*. Redox can be redefined with electrons in mind.

Reduction occurs when a chemical species accepts electrons in a reaction

The term 'species' means atoms, ions, molecules or free radicals. The species are the particles in chemical reactions which, in this case, gain or lose electrons. The electrons can come from an electric current as in *figure 2.3*:

$$Cu^{2+}(aq) \; + \; 2e^- \longrightarrow Cu(s)$$
$$\llcorner reduced \underline{\hspace{4cm}} \uparrow$$

The electrons can come from other atoms of more reactive elements, which themselves become ions. Elements which release *electrons*, becoming *positive* ions in the process, are said to be more **electropositive** than the metals whose ions receive the electrons. For example, copper is less electropositive than magnesium:

$$Cu^{2+}(aq) \; + \; Mg(s) \longrightarrow Cu(s) \; + \; Mg^{2+}(aq)$$
$$\llcorner reduced \underline{\hspace{4cm}} \uparrow$$

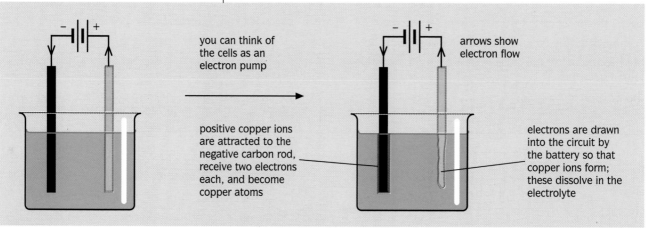

you can think of the cells as an electron pump

arrows show electron flow

positive copper ions are attracted to the negative carbon rod, receive two electrons each, and become copper atoms

electrons are drawn into the circuit by the battery so that copper ions form; these dissolve in the electrolyte

● **Figure 2.2** The negative electrode (cathode) is made of carbon, and becomes coated with metal during electrolysis. The positive electrode (anode) is made of copper, and corrodes away during electrolysis.

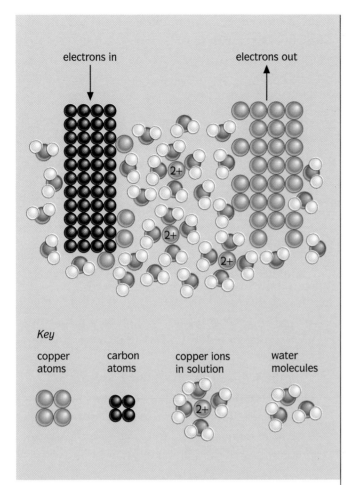

Key

| copper atoms | carbon atoms | copper ions in solution | water molecules |

● **Figure 2.3** This is what happens during the electrolysis shown in *figure 2.2*. However, the electrons are not shown. Try to imagine how they are flowing, where they are lost, and where they are gained by the particles involved.

Another way to put this is that copper is *more electronegative* than magnesium.

Oxidation occurs when a chemical species loses electrons in a reaction

During electrolysis, electrons can be pulled into the positive electrode:

$$Cu(s) \longrightarrow Cu^{2+}(aq) + 2e^-$$
$$\underbrace{\qquad}_{\text{oxidised}}$$

In other reactions, electrons can be pulled away by atoms or molecules of more electronegative elements, which become negative ions:

$$2Fe(s) + 3Cl_2(g) \longrightarrow 2Fe^{3+}(aq) + 6Cl^-(aq)$$
$$\underbrace{\qquad\qquad}_{\text{oxidised}}$$

Box 2A

Many textbooks include this memory help:
OIL RIG
It works, so we will use it too.

Oxidation Is Loss of electrons from a species.
Reduction Is Gain of electrons by a species.

SAQ 2.3

What is oxidised and what is reduced in the reactions below?

Justify your answers in terms of electron transfer.

a $2Cu(s) + I_2(g) \longrightarrow 2CuI(s)$

b $Fe^{3+}(aq) + e^- \longrightarrow Fe^{2+}(aq)$

c $Fe(s) + Cu^{2+}(aq) \longrightarrow Fe^{2+}(aq) + Cu(s)$

d $2Mg(s) + O_2(g) \longrightarrow 2MgO(s)$

e $Cu^{2+}(aq) + Ag(s) \longrightarrow Cu^+(aq) + Ag^+(aq)$

Redox redefined

Chemists like big ideas that include many substances. For example, they find it useful to extend definitions to widen the base of materials that can be considered as acids. The same is true about redox reactions – the wider the field to which it applies, the more use it can be.

To get round this, chemists have therefore developed another definition for oxidation and reduction – to widen the base of redox reactions that we come across.

This is the system.

■ Each reacting species – atom, molecule or ion – can be given an oxidation number. This number can be positive, negative or zero.
■ Oxidation is an increase in oxidation number.
■ Reduction is a decrease in oxidation number.

We shall now consider an example. When magnesium burns in nitrogen, the oxidation number of magnesium increases from 0 to +2. Magnesium is oxidised. At the same time, the oxidation number of nitrogen drops from 0 to −3. Nitrogen is reduced.

$$\overset{0}{3Mg(s)} + \overset{0}{N_2(g)} \xrightarrow{\text{oxidation numbers}} \overset{+2 \; -3}{Mg_3N_2(s)}$$
$$\underset{\text{oxidised}}{\big|} \underbrace{\qquad\qquad}_{\text{reduced}}$$

Rules concerning oxidation numbers

This system is fine if you know what the oxidation numbers are. You can work them out. There are some basic rules to follow.

1 Atoms of elements that are not combined with any other element have an oxidation number of zero.

The oxidation number of sodium atoms in sodium metal is 0. The oxidation number of chlorine atoms in chlorine gas, Cl_2, is 0.

SAQ 2.4
What is the oxidation number of a uranium atom?

2 Ions of elements have oxidation numbers equal to the charge on the ion.

The oxidation number of sodium ions, Na^+, is $+1$. The oxidation number of aluminium ions, Al^{3+}, is $+3$. The oxidation number of chlorine ions, Cl^-, is -1.

SAQ 2.5
What are the oxidation numbers of the oxide ion, O^{2-}, and the hydrogen ion, H^+?

3 The oxidation number of hydrogen in nearly all of its compounds is $+1$.

The exceptions for hydrogen are the metal hydrides. The oxidation number of hydrogen in such hydrides as LiH and AlH_3 is -1. (This comes under one of the rules above. Which is it?)

4 The oxidation number of oxygen in nearly all of its compounds is -2.

One exception for oxygen is in oxygen fluoride, OF_2, in which oxygen, being more electropositive than fluorine, has an oxidation number of $+2$. Another exception for oxygen are the peroxides, containing the covalent bonds $-O-O-$.

5 In a molecule, the sum of the oxidation numbers of its atoms is 0.

In water, H_2O, the sum of oxidation numbers $= [2 \times (+1)] + (-2) = 0$. In carbon dioxide, CO_2, the sum of the oxidation numbers $= 0$. Since each oxygen atom contributes -2, the oxidation number of carbon must be $= +4$.

SAQ 2.6
What is the oxidation number of carbon in carbon monoxide, CO?

SAQ 2.7
What is the oxidation number of oxygen in hydrogen peroxide, H_2O_2, structure H–O–O–H? (Use rules 3 and 5 to make the calculation.)

6 In ions, the sum of the oxidation numbers equals the size and sign of the charge on the ion itself.

In the hydroxide ion, OH^-, the oxidation numbers are -2 (for oxygen) and $+1$ (for hydrogen.) This gives a total of $-2 + 1 = -1$, the charge on the ion itself.

In the sulphate ion, SO_4^{2-}, the sum of the oxidation numbers must be -2. Since there are four oxygen atoms in each ion, each with an oxidation number of -2 (making -8), the oxidation number of the sulphur atom must be $+6$.

SAQ 2.8
What is the oxidation number of carbon in the carbonate ion, CO_3^{2-}?

7 In any substance, the more electronegative atom always has the negative oxidation number.

In sulphur dioxide, SO_2, oxygen is more electronegative than sulphur. This means that the oxidation number of sulphur *must* be positive. Its value is $+4$. (Check this and make sure it is correct.)

Fluorine is the most electronegative of all elements. The fluoride ion has the charge -1. Thus in iodine fluoride, IF, the oxidation number of fluorine is -1. By rule 5, the oxidation of iodine in this compound is $+1$, not -1 as it is in iodides of metals such as potassium iodide, KI.

SAQ 2.9
What is the oxidation number of each of the other elements in these fluorides?

   ClF CaF_2 XeF_4

Box 2B Calculations and names

Here is one way of calculating oxidation numbers, using algebra. You may prefer a method of your own. If it works, use it.

Calculate the oxidation number of chromium in the dichromate ion, $Cr_2O_7^{2-}$

Let n = the oxidation number of chromium in this ion. From the formula and the charge on the ion, we can write

$$(2 \times n) + [7 \times (-2)] = -2$$

there are 2 Cr atoms

the overall charge of the ion is -2

there are 7 oxygen atoms, each with an oxidation number of -2

Therefore

$$2n - 14 = -2$$
$$2n = +12$$
$$n = +6$$

In the green powder, chromium oxide, Cr_2O_3, the oxidation number is different. From the formula we can write

$$2n + [3 \times (-2)] = 0$$
$$2n = +6$$
$$n = +3$$

In the ion $Cr_2O_7^{2-}$ the oxidation state of chromium is $+6$, but in Cr_2O_3 it is $+3$. Many elements, such as sulphur and manganese, have more than one oxidation state. This helps to name the many compounds that contain these elements. This is illustrated in the table below.

Formula of species	Oxidation number of manganese	Name
MnO_4^-	$+7$	manganate(VII) ion (spoken as manganate seven ion)
MnO_4^{2-}	$+6$	manganate(VI) ion

(Note: the ending 'ate' indicates the presence of oxygen in the ion.)

Heavy metal, a salt and battery

You need portable electricity supplies for some of the finer things in life – calculators, Walkmans, second-hand cars (*figure 2.4*). In each case a battery of cells supplies a direct current. In each case redox reactions supply a flow of electrons. We make sure the electrons flow through something useful, like a chip or a starter motor, so that they work for us.

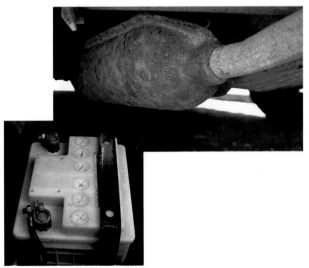

● **Figure 2.4** Redox reactions in the battery get the car started. Redox reactions in the bodywork will eventually stop it.

In a car battery (*figure 2.5*) the electrons are liberated from sheets of lead, creating lead ions.

$$Pb(s) \longrightarrow Pb^{2+}(aq) + 2e^-$$

The electrons travel through thick copper wires to the starter motor, kick it into motion, and return to the battery to plates of lead(IV) oxide. A reaction occurs, which again produces lead ions. Hydrogen ions from the sulphuric acid electrolyte in the battery also play their part:

$$PbO_2(s) + 2e^- + 4H^+(aq) \longrightarrow Pb^{2+}(aq) + 2H_2O(l)$$

SAQ 2.10

Redox reactions produce the power in a car battery. Work out what is reduced and what is the reducing agent in the reactions in a car battery, discussed above, using the ideas of electron loss or gain and oxidation numbers.

In a rusting car body, electrons also flow. This time, however, they do nothing useful. They simply contribute to the conversion of steel to soft brown sludge. Redox reactions let Nature reclaim its own.

$$Fe(s) \longrightarrow Fe^{2+}(aq) + 2e^-$$
$$H_2O(l) + \tfrac{1}{2}O_2(aq) + 2e^- \longrightarrow 2OH^-(aq)$$
$$Fe^{2+}(aq) + 2OH^-(aq) \longrightarrow Fe(OH)_2(s)$$

Redox continues, influenced by oxygen dissolved in the water. Eventually hydrated iron(III) oxide, $Fe_2O_3nH_2O(s)$ is formed – what we know as rust. Again you should be able to deduce what is oxidised and what is reduced.

Corrosion occurs in most electrical cells. A metal ionises in solution, releasing electrons into a circuit. The example in *figure 2.6* shows a piece of copper in a solution of one of its own salts. Some copper atoms dissolve in the copper sulphate solution, forming copper ions:

$$Cu(s) \longrightarrow Cu^{2+}(aq) + 2e^-$$

However, the reverse occurs as well. Copper ions in contact with the metal acquire electrons and deposit on the metal:

$$Cu^{2+}(aq) + 2e^- \longrightarrow Cu(s)$$

This is a give-and-take situation. The reaction goes both ways until a balance is established. The two-way arrows are used to show this:

$$Cu(s) \rightleftharpoons Cu^{2+}(aq) + 2e^-$$

This two-way balance is called an **equilibrium**. It is a dynamic situation, one of constant interchange.

In this example, the balance is established when there are slightly more copper atoms on the plate than there were before, and slightly fewer copper ions in solution. This is accompanied by an imbalance of charge. The extra copper ions that settle on the plate need electrons. Enough are available within the rod to bind the copper ions to the rod. However, since there are not enough to provide each copper ion with two electrons, the plate has a positive

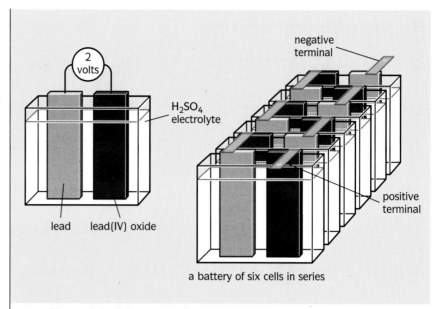

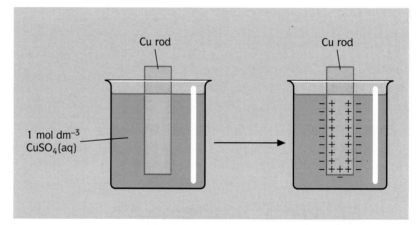

● *Figure 2.5* This battery of six 2 volt cells in series supplies an electrical potential of 12 volts – enough to drive a current of over 30 amperes through the starter motor.

● *Figure 2.6* A sheet of copper metal in aqueous copper sulphate. Some copper atoms are entering the copper sulphate solution, leaving electrons behind. At the same time, some copper ions are leaving the solution, gaining electrons from the copper rod and forming atoms at its surface.

charge (*figure 2.7*). There is a balancing negative charge in solution near the plate where there is a slight excess of negatively charged ions in solution.

Figure 2.7 leaves out water molecules, unlike *figure 2.8*. The latter shows how copper ions are going into solution, and vice versa. You cannot tell which!

The electrical imbalance creates a voltage. This happens every time an electrode is dipped into a solution of its ions. There is a separation of charge, and an electrical potential is established. It is called the **electrode potential**. Some more examples are shown in *figure 2.9*.

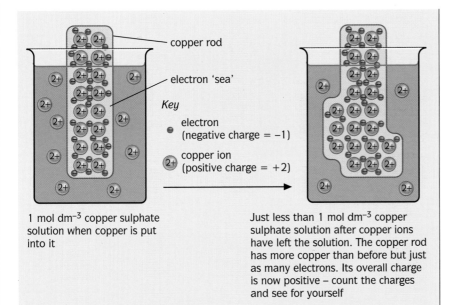

1 mol dm^{-3} copper sulphate solution when copper is put into it

Just less than 1 mol dm^{-3} copper sulphate solution after copper ions have left the solution. The copper rod has more copper than before but just as many electrons. Its overall charge is now positive – count the charges and see for yourself

● **Figure 2.7** This is one way of showing how the copper rod becomes positive – count the charges for yourself and see.

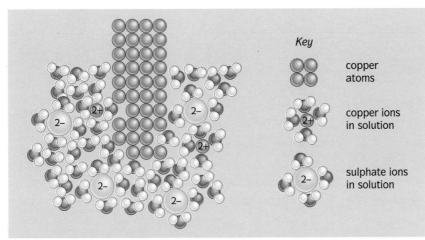

● **Figure 2.8** An imaginary snapshot of the equilibrium being achieved, with copper ions leaving the rod, other copper ions joining it, and sulphate ions in solution. Compare the illustration with *figure 2.7*. Use both to help you to imagine what is happening.

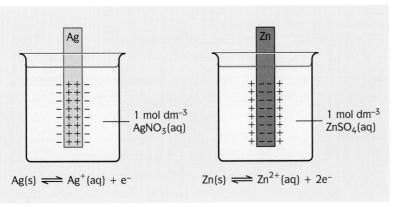

$Ag(s) \rightleftharpoons Ag^+(aq) + e^-$

1 mol dm^{-3} AgNO$_3$(aq)

$Zn(s) \rightleftharpoons Zn^{2+}(aq) + 2e^-$

1 mol dm^{-3} ZnSO$_4$(aq)

● **Figure 2.9**

Reactivity

We regard sodium as highly reactive. We can see it oxidise immediately when its surface is cut and exposed to the atmosphere. Sodium reacts vigorously with cold water, producing hydrogen; magnesium reacts slowly. Magnesium is less reactive than sodium, but more reactive than copper, which does not react with cold water at all.

Iron comes between the two. Iron will displace copper ions in solution, forming copper metal and leaving ions of iron in solution:

$$Fe(s) + Cu^{2+}(aq)$$
$$\longrightarrow Fe^{2+}(aq) + Cu(s)$$

However, iron will not displace magnesium ions from solution – quite the reverse, in fact, as magnesium metal replaces iron ions:

$$Mg(s) + Fe^{2+}(aq)$$
$$\longrightarrow Mg^{2+}(aq) + Fe(s)$$

Gold does not oxidise in air, does not react with water or even steam, and does not replace the ions of any of these metals in solution. Gold is very unreactive. Ancient gold jewellery has survived intact for centuries in the warm, salty, corrosive seas of the Mediterranean. A simple reactivity series for metals has gold firmly at the bottom:

Most reactive K
Na
Ca
Mg
Al
Zn
Fe
Pb
Cu
Hg
Ag
Pt
Least reactive Au

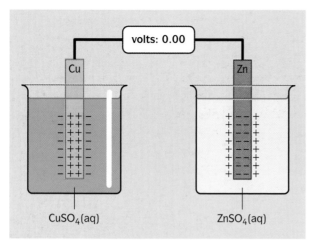

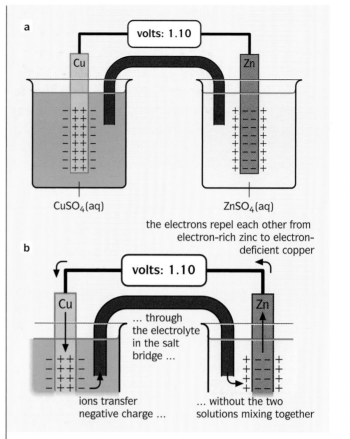

● **Figure 2.10** An incomplete attempt to form a whole cell from two half-cells.

Half-cells

Each of the examples in *figure 2.9* shows a half-cell. This is because any two of them can be joined to form a whole cell – one that could supply an electron flow for us to use. *Figure 2.10* shows an attempt to link two half-cells to make a whole cell. It fails because the circuit is incomplete.

Figure 2.11 shows how a 'salt bridge' completes the circuit. The salt bridge is a tube containing (or a strip of filter paper soaked in) an aqueous solution of a good electrolyte, for example potassium nitrate, $KNO_3(aq)$. This enables charge to be transferred without the solutions of zinc sulphate and copper sulphate being mixed. (**Electrolytes** are solutions which decompose at the electrodes when an electric current passes through. However, there is no decomposition in the salt bridge.) The electrons pass through the wire, whilst the ions move along the salt bridge.

Non-metal half-cells

It is convenient to make half-cells of non-metals such as chlorine and hydrogen. A hydrogen half-cell would consist of a layer of hydrogen atoms in contact with hydrogen ions in solution, just as a copper electrode consists of copper atoms in contact with copper ions in solution.

We have to make an electrode of hydrogen so that we can use it under normal laboratory

● **Figure 2.11**
a A salt bridge completes the circuit. This cell is called a Daniell cell, after its inventor.
b The flow of negative charge (electrons).

conditions. Solidifying it at $-260\,°C$ is not on so we create a layer of immobile hydrogen atoms in contact with hydrogen ions in solution. Just one layer of hydrogen atoms will do. We use platinum to hold the layer of hydrogen atoms. Platinum adsorbs molecules of gases onto its surface, that is, it holds them fast when they come in contact with the metal. If hydrogen is bubbled through an acidic solution onto platinum, molecules of hydrogen are attracted to it. The molecules dissociate (split up) and the atoms formed bond to the platinum surface. This forms a layer of hydrogen atoms on a conductor, in contact with hydrogen ions in solution – a hydrogen electrode (*figure 2.12*).

A hydrogen ion, H^+, is actually a proton. Protons do not float around on their own – they are too reactive. In aqueous solutions they combine with water molecules to form the charged species H_3O^+. This is called an **oxonium ion**, and

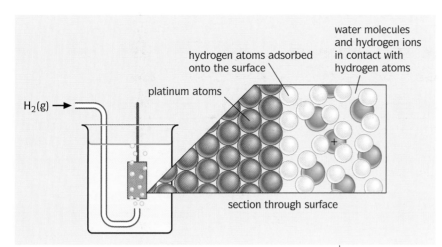

• **Figure 2.12** A hydrogen electrode. The so-called hydrogen ion is formed from a proton combining with a water molecule to form H_3O^+.

is equivalent to a water molecule giving a hydrogen ion a piggy-back!

In a commercial hydrogen electrode, the platinum is not shiny, but black. The surface of the electrode is porous and pitted, a bit like a miniature sponge. This creates a very large surface area for the hydrogen to be adsorbed onto.

Setting standards

The electrode potentials for cells need to be known in order to design cells and other redox systems. Several factors can affect the potential, for example the temperature, the atmospheric pressure, the concentration of electrolyte and the purity of the metal.

We assume that if we refer to copper or zinc we mean the pure metal. *Box 2C* explains what the standard conditions should be.

Figure 2.14 shows how the standard electrode potential for copper would be measured under standard conditions. (What are these conditions for the copper/copper sulphate half-cell?) The experimental value is $+0.34\,V$. The copper is positive in relation to the hydrogen electrode – not the case with most metals. A set of standard electrode potentials is given in *table 2.1*. Note the convention for writing the half-cell equation:

$$\text{oxidised form} + n\text{e}^- \rightleftharpoons \text{reduced form}$$

Box 2C

Standard electrode potentials are given the symbol $E^{\ominus}(298)$. E stands for electrode potential, $^{\ominus}$ means standard, and 298 is the temperature in kelvin.

Standard electrode potentials need a benchmark for making comparisons, in other words a zero value. This is provided by a standard hydrogen electrode, assumed to

have a standard electrode potential of 0.00 volts (V). A standard hydrogen electrode is illustrated in *figure 2.13*. Note that the conditions should be maintained so that the temperature is 298 K, there is one atmosphere pressure (101 kPa), in an acidic solution where the concentration of hydrogen ions is $1\,mol\,dm^{-3}$.

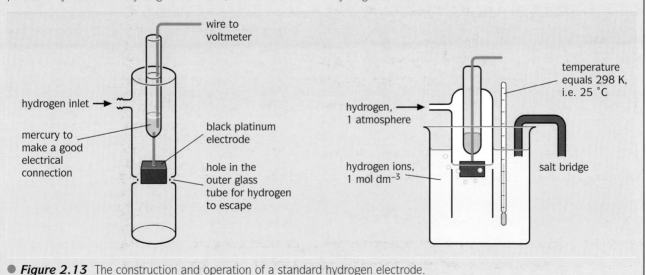

• **Figure 2.13** The construction and operation of a standard hydrogen electrode.

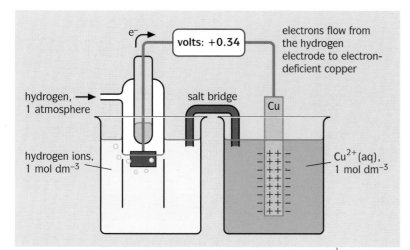

● **Figure 2.14** Experimental set-up for measuring the standard redox potential for copper.

					$E^{\ominus}(298)/V$
$F_2(g)$	+	$2e^-$	$\rightleftharpoons$	$2F^-(aq)$	+ 2.87
$Au^{3+}(aq)$	+	$3e^-$	$\rightleftharpoons$	$Au(s)$	+ 1.42
$Cl_2(aq)$	+	$2e^-$	$\rightleftharpoons$	$2Cl^-(aq)$	+ 1.36
$Br_2(aq)$	+	$2e^-$	$\rightleftharpoons$	$2Br^-(aq)$	+ 1.07
$Ag^+(aq)$	+	e^-	$\rightleftharpoons$	$Ag(s)$	+ 0.80
$I_2(aq)$	+	$2e^-$	$\rightleftharpoons$	$2I^-(aq)$	+ 0.54
$Cu^+(aq)$	+	e^-	$\rightleftharpoons$	$Cu(s)$	+ 0.52
$Cu^{2+}(aq)$	+	$2e^-$	$\rightleftharpoons$	$Cu(s)$	+ 0.34
$2H^+(aq)$	**+**	**$2e^-$**	**$\rightleftharpoons$**	**$H_2(g)$**	**+ 0.00**
$Fe^{3+}(aq)$	+	$3e^-$	$\rightleftharpoons$	$Fe(s)$	− 0.04
$Pb^{2+}(aq)$	+	$2e^-$	$\rightleftharpoons$	$Pb(s)$	− 0.13
$Sn^{2+}(aq)$	+	$2e^-$	$\rightleftharpoons$	$Sn(s)$	− 0.14
$Ni^{2+}(aq)$	+	$2e^-$	$\rightleftharpoons$	$Ni(s)$	− 0.26
$Fe^{2+}(aq)$	+	$2e^-$	$\rightleftharpoons$	$Fe(s)$	− 0.44
$Zn^{2+}(aq)$	+	$2e^-$	$\rightleftharpoons$	$Zn(s)$	− 0.76
$Cr^{2+}(aq)$	+	$2e^-$	$\rightleftharpoons$	$Cr(s)$	− 0.90
$Al^{3+}(aq)$	+	$3e^-$	$\rightleftharpoons$	$Al(s)$	− 1.67
$Mg^{2+}(aq)$	+	$2e^-$	$\rightleftharpoons$	$Mg(s)$	− 2.37
$Na^+(aq)$	+	e^-	$\rightleftharpoons$	$Na(s)$	− 2.71
$Ca^{2+}(aq)$	+	$2e^-$	$\rightleftharpoons$	$Ca(s)$	− 2.84
$K^+(aq)$	+	e^-	$\rightleftharpoons$	$K(s)$	− 2.93
$Li^+(aq)$	+	e^-	$\rightleftharpoons$	$Li(s)$	− 3.04

● **Table 2.1** Standard electrode potentials for some selected elements, shown in volts (V)

Standard cell potentials

Two standard half-cells, combined to form a complete cell, provide standard cell potentials. The standard cell potential for the Daniell cell is 1.1 V when measured with a voltmeter of very high or infinite resistance, for example a potentiometer.

The standard cell potential is calculated from the standard redox potentials using the following data:

$$Cu^{2+}(aq) + 2e^- \rightleftharpoons Cu(s) \qquad +0.34\,V$$
$$(2.1)$$
$$Zn^{2+}(aq) + 2e^- \rightleftharpoons Zn(s) \qquad -0.76\,V$$
$$(2.2)$$

When the cell is producing a current, copper atoms are depositing on the copper plate, as represented by *reaction 2.1*. At the same time zinc metal is going into solution, forming zinc ions – the reverse of *reaction 2.2*. This can be rewritten as follows:

$$Zn(s) \rightleftharpoons Zn^{2+}(aq) + 2e^- \qquad +0.76\,V \;(2.3)$$

Note the reversal of sign for the voltage, −0.76 to +0.76 V. Now adding *reaction 2.1* to *reaction 2.3* summarises the reactions occurring:

$$Zn(s) + Cu^{2+}(aq) \longrightarrow Zn^{2+}(aq) + Cu(s)$$

We add the voltages as well. The overall voltage, or cell potential for the reaction, is +0.34 V + 0.76 V = +1.10 V.

A quick way to obtain the same result is to use *table 2.1* directly. Simply work out $\Delta E^{\ominus}$, the difference between the two voltages. Thus a cell made from standard silver and magnesium cells would create a voltage of +0.80 V + 2.37 V = +3.17 V.

SAQ 2.11 _____

Which would be the positive terminal in a standard silver and magnesium cell? Which metal would be oxidised in this cell? Which would be reduced?

Ions with different oxidation states

So far we have dealt with metals in solutions of their metal ions, and non-metals in solution with their non-metal ions. There is a third type to consider – ions of the same element but in different oxidation states. The d-block elements provide these ions. For example, iron has two oxidation states, Fe^{2+} and Fe^{3+}, of which Fe^{2+} is

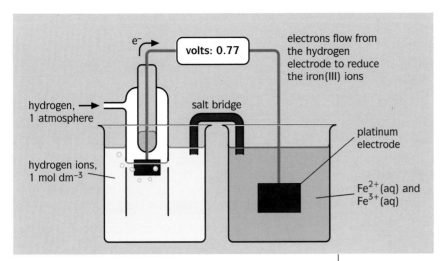

● **Figure 2.15** Using a hydrogen electrode to measure the standard redox potential of a mixed ion system.

the lower oxidation state since a gain of an electron by an Fe^{3+} ion would give an Fe^{2+} ion:

$$Fe^{3+}(aq) + e^- \rightleftharpoons Fe^{2+}(aq)$$

The voltage required to initiate this change can be measured using a hydrogen electrode as before. Note that this time the two species (Fe^{2+} and Fe^{3+}) are not in separate layers or phases – they are mixed together in solution, as shown in *figure 2.15*.

The electrode potentials of some other standard mixed ion solutions are given in *table 2.2*.

					$E^{\ominus}(298)/V$
$Co^{3+}(aq)$	+	e^-	$\rightleftharpoons$	$Co^{2+}(aq)$	$+1.82$
$Pb^{4+}(aq)$	+	$2e^-$	$\rightleftharpoons$	$Pb^{2+}(aq)$	$+1.69$
$Mn^{3+}(aq)$	+	e^-	$\rightleftharpoons$	$Mn^{2+}(aq)$	$+1.51$
$Fe^{3+}(aq)$	+	e^-	$\rightleftharpoons$	$Fe^{2+}(aq)$	$+0.77$
$Cu^{2+}(aq)$	+	e^-	$\rightleftharpoons$	$Cu^+(aq)$	$+0.15$
$Sn^{4+}(aq)$	+	$2e^-$	$\rightleftharpoons$	$Sn^{2+}(aq)$	$+0.15$
$Cr^{3+}(aq)$	+	e^-	$\rightleftharpoons$	$Cr^{2+}(aq)$	-0.41

● **Table 2.2** Standard electrode potentials in volts (V) for ions of the same element but in different oxidation states

Cell statements – an international convention

This is the cell statement for the Daniell cell:

$$Zn(s)|Zn^{2+}(aq) \overset{\shortmid}{\underset{\shortmid}{\mid}} Cu^{2+}(aq)|Cu(s)$$

■ The more positive half-cell, $Cu^{2+}(aq)|Cu(s)$, is placed on the right.

■ The half-cell on the left, $Zn(s)|Zn^{2+}(aq)$, must represent an oxidation (in this case Zn losing electrons).

■ The half-cell on the right, $Cu^{2+}(aq)|Cu(s)$, must represent a reduction (in this case Cu^{2+} gaining electrons).

The cell statement for measuring the standard electrode potential of a half-cell is always written with the hydrogen electrode on the left:

$$Pt|H_2(g)|H^+(aq) \overset{\shortmid}{\underset{\shortmid}{\mid}} Zn^{2+}(aq)|Zn(s)$$
$$E^{\ominus}(298) = -0.76\,V$$

Note that the inert (that is, unreacting) electrode of platinum comes first, reflecting the order of materials in the hydrogen electrode.

The vertical line, |, represents a so-called 'phase boundary', i.e. where one phase, in this case the solid platinum, is in contact with another, the adsorbed hydrogen gas. Try to identify the remaining phase boundaries in the cell statements above.

The double broken lines, $\overset{\shortmid}{\underset{\shortmid}{\;}}$, represent a salt bridge. The other symbol to use is a comma, where you have two ions in solution together, as shown below.

$$Pt|H_2(g)|H^+(aq) \overset{\shortmid}{\underset{\shortmid}{\mid}} Fe^{3+}(aq), Fe^{2+}(aq)|Pt$$
$$E^{\ominus}(298) = 0.77\,V$$

This is the cell that is shown in *figure 2.15* – make the comparison to help you understand it. There is a symmetry in the order which should help you write other cell statements, as shown below:

Pt—reduced—oxidised—bridge—oxidised—reduced—Pt
    species   species   species   species

Calculating cell voltage: an example

Write the cell statement for an iron/aluminium cell using the following standard redox potentials. Then calculate the voltage of the cell and the direction in which electrons would flow.

a $Al^{3+}(aq) + 3e^- \rightleftharpoons Al(s)$ $E^{\ominus}(298) = -1.67\,V$
b $Fe^{2+}(aq) + 2e^- \rightleftharpoons Fe(s)$ $E^{\ominus}(298) = -0.44\,V$

A way to answer

The more positive redox potential is that for iron. (It is not so negative as the redox potential of aluminium.) Put this on the *right* of the cell statement, with the reduced species of iron, the metal, at the end:

$$\text{............................} \;\Vert\; \mathrm{Fe^{2+}(aq)} \,|\, \mathrm{Fe(s)}$$

Now complete the cell statement, beginning with the reduced species of aluminium, the metal:

$$\mathrm{Al(s)} \,|\, \mathrm{Al^{3+}(aq)} \;\Vert\; \mathrm{Fe^{2+}(aq)} \,|\, \mathrm{Fe(s)}$$

The total potential of the cell, the standard cell potential, is given by the rule

$$E^{\ominus}(298)_{\text{cell}} = E^{\ominus}(298)_{\text{right}} - E^{\ominus}(298)_{\text{left}}$$

so

$$\begin{aligned} E^{\ominus}(298)_{\text{cell}} &= -0.44\,\mathrm{V} - (-1.67)\,\mathrm{V} \\ &= +1.23\,\mathrm{V} \end{aligned}$$

The positive value, $+1.23\,\mathrm{V}$, indicates that the cell will produce a potential, that is, electrons will flow and reactions will occur. The direction of electron flow is from left to right, from aluminium to iron. *Figure 2.16* will help you understand why.

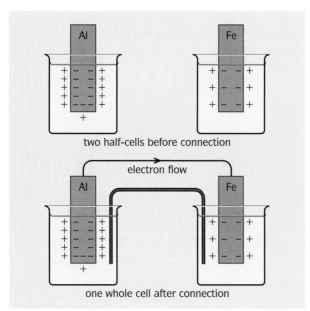

● **Figure 2.16** Aluminium has a more negative redox potential than iron. This means that more free electrons build up on the aluminium plate than on the iron. When the salt bridge and conducting wire are in place, electrons flow from where there are more to where there are less.

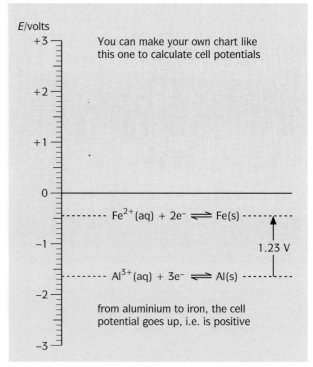

● **Figure 2.17** An electrode potential diagram, drawn to scale. You can get a good idea of relative potentials using rough-and-ready sketches.

Figure 2.17 shows an electrode potential diagram for aluminium and iron(II). This will help you visualise the situation and to calculate cell potentials.

Will it react or won't it?

It is useful to be able to make predictions about reactions. Suppose a copper lightning conductor was to be connected to an iron rod buried in the ground as shown in *figure 2.18*. Would the iron rust faster as a result? Would the copper corrode in the rain?

Let's assume that the iron will not corrode, in which case the tendency to form iron(II) ions will not be encouraged by the copper. We can write a cell statement for this assumption as follows:

$$\text{............................} \;\Vert\; \mathrm{Fe^{2+}(aq)} \,|\, \mathrm{Fe(s)}$$

Then

$$\mathrm{Cu(s)} \,|\, \mathrm{Cu^{2+}(aq)} \;\Vert\; \mathrm{Fe^{2+}(aq)} \,|\, \mathrm{Fe(s)}$$

If our assumption is correct, then electrons will flow from the copper half-cell to the iron half-cell. We can check by calculating the *sign* of the cell

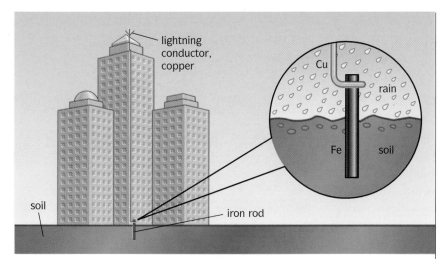

● **Figure 2.18** A lightning conductor buried in the ground. How will the redox reactions be affected?

potential. If it is positive, the reaction goes. If not, it doesn't. Now

$$E^{\ominus}(298)_{cell} = E^{\ominus}(298)_{right} - E^{\ominus}(298)_{left}$$

so

$$E^{\ominus}(298)_{cell} = -0.44 - (+0.34)\,V$$
$$= -0.77\,V$$

The negative result shows that our cell would not react as written in the cell statement. The reverse would be the case, as shown below:

$$Fe(s)\,|\,Fe^{2+}(aq)\,\overset{!!}{!!}\,Cu^{2+}(aq)\,|\,Cu(s)$$

In this cell, $E^{\ominus}_{cell}$ is positive ($+0.77\,V$). Electrons would flow from iron to the right, and iron(II) ions would be produced – the first stage in its rusting. The iron connected to the copper lightning conductor would corrode away sooner than an unconnected one. It would be better to bury the copper itself in the ground.

Suppose a researcher was investigating the ability of nickel to reduce cobalt ions in solution. He or she might save a lot of experimental work by doing some calculations first. Here are two reactions proposed by the researcher:

a $Co^{2+}(aq) + Ni(s) \longrightarrow Ni^{2+}(aq) + Co(s)$
b $2Co^{3+}(aq) + Ni(s) \longrightarrow 2Co^{2+}(aq) + Ni^{2+}(aq)$

Could these reactions occur?

We shall test reaction **a**. The reaction consists of two so-called 'half-reactions' combined together, i.e.

$$Ni(s) \qquad\qquad \longrightarrow Ni^{2+}(aq) + 2e^{-}$$
$$Co^{2+}(aq) + 2e^{-} \qquad \longrightarrow Co(s)$$

Check by adding	$Ni(s) \;\;+ Co^{2+}(aq) \longrightarrow Ni^{2+}(aq) + Co(s)$

(The electrons cancel out – they are produced and used again.) Now we write the cell statement for the reaction we imagine might happen, i.e., from left to right as in the equation:

$$Ni(s)\,|\,Ni^{2+}(aq)\,\overset{!!}{!!}\,Co^{2+}(aq)\,|\,Co(s)$$

Since

$$E^{\ominus}(298)_{cell}$$
$$= E^{\ominus}(298)_{right} - E^{\ominus}(298)_{left}$$

Then

$$E^{\ominus}(298)_{cell} = -0.28\,V - (-0.25)\,V$$
$$= -0.03\,V$$

The negative value indicates that the reaction would *not* happen as imagined.

SAQ 2.12

Will nickel reduce cobalt(III) ions to cobalt(II) ions? Make calculations and decide whether this reduction would occur. The standard redox potential for this reduction is shown below. What are your first thoughts – before the calculations begin?

$$Co^{3+}(aq) + e^{-} \longrightarrow Co^{2+}(aq)$$
$$E^{\ominus}(298) = +1.82\,V$$

Prediction and practicality – a note of caution

The predictions we have been making tell us what *can* happen, but not *when*. Redox calculations show that hydrogen gas and oxygen gas will react, they do not tell you the rate of reaction. Indeed, at 298 K the rate is so slow as to be virtually non-existent. You can safely leave a sealed bottle of hydrogen and oxygen around the house for centuries if conditions are kept the same.

Redox calculations take no account of activation energies. (The **activation energy** of a reaction is the minimum initial input of energy required to make the reaction take place.) The enormous amounts of energy locked up in the liquid hydrogen and liquid oxygen fuel of the Saturn V launchers, which took men into Earth orbit for the lunar missions, needed a spark of energy to start the reaction.

More down to Earth, fuel cells lower activation energies so that reactions can occur at room temperatures. Hydrogen gas and oxygen gas can react together to form water, exchanging electrons in the process. A fuel cell using hydrogen and oxygen can channel these electrons to produce considerable amounts of energy. Every litre ($1\,dm^3$) of water produced in the fuel cell is accompanied by the production of over $13\,000\,kJ$ of electrical energy, enough to keep a 100 watt light bulb going for over 36 hours.

There is another precaution to note. Redox potentials are quoted under standard conditions. In reality, conditions are seldom standard, and when they are, they change as reactions proceed. In the Daniell cell for example, the concentration of copper ions decreases and the concentration of zinc ions increases, slowly reducing the voltage below the normal working level.

More redox reactions and how to construct equations

The redox potential diagram in *figure 2.19* indicates the relative oxidising strengths of several chemical systems. At times you will need to be able to write equations for reactions that occur between two of these systems. Here is an example.

What reaction occurs if an $Fe(s)/Fe^{2+}(aq)$ half-cell is connected to an $MnO_4^-(aq)/MnO_2(s)$ half-cell? Write the equation for the reaction that occurs.

Examination of the chart shows that electrons will flow to the most positive half-cell, $MnO_4^-(aq)/MnO_2(s)$. This gain of electrons will cause a reduction. The half equation will be

$$MnO_4^-(aq) + 4H^+(aq) + 3e^- \longrightarrow MnO_2(s) + 2H_2O(l) \qquad (2.4)$$

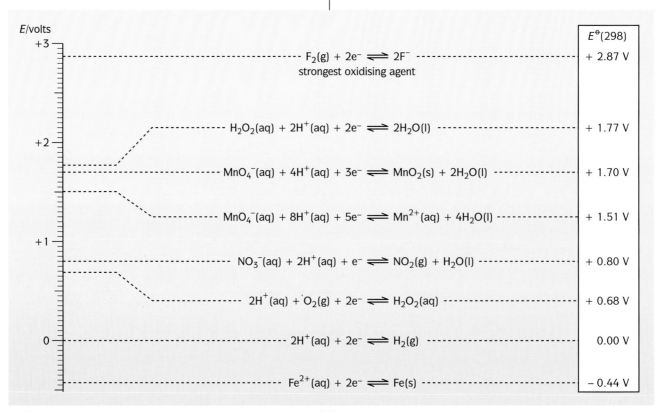

● *Figure 2.19* A redox potential diagram for some useful oxidising agents.

The electrons are supplied by the more negative half-cell:

$$Fe(s) \longrightarrow Fe^{2+}(aq) + 2e^- \qquad (2.5)$$

However, examination of the electron 'balance sheet' shows that there is not an equal supply of electrons as the equations stand. *Equation 2.4* requires three electrons, *equation 2.5* supplies only two electrons. However, if we multiply *equation 2.4* by 2 (to receive 6e⁻), and *equation 2.5* by 3 (to produce 6e⁻), the equations *will* balance:

$$2MnO_4^-(aq) + 8H^+(aq) + 6e^-$$
$$\longrightarrow 2MnO_2(s) + 4H_2O(l) \qquad (2.6)$$

$$3Fe(s) \longrightarrow 3Fe^{2+}(aq) + 6e^- \qquad (2.7)$$

We can now add *equations 2.6* and *2.7*, which eliminates the six electrons on each side of the equation. The final equation is therefore:

$$2MnO_4^-(aq) + 8H^+(aq) + 3Fe(s)$$
$$\longrightarrow 3Fe^{2+}(aq) + 2MnO_2(s) + 4H_2O(l)$$

This is not the sort of equation you would want to learn parrot fashion. It is much more important to be able to work it out. Try writing equations for the reactions that would occur if other half-cells were connected.

SAQ 2.13

Write the equation for the reaction that would occur if chromium(II) ions, $Cr^{2+}(aq)$, were added to acidified manganate(VII) ions, $MnO_4^-(aq)$ with $H^+(aq)$.

Loss of concentration?

Let's hope not – but it does happen in the best of cells. So does gain in concentration. What changes occur in the concentrations of electrolytes as a Daniell cell discharges? A look at the cell statement can answer this question:

$$Zn(s)|Zn^{2+}(aq) \overset{||}{||} Cu^{2+}(aq)|Cu(s)$$
$$E^{\ominus}(298)_{cell} = +1.10\,V$$

Since $E^{\ominus}(298)_{cell}$ is positive, we know that electrons flow so as to promote the formation of zinc ions in solution, and to reduce copper ions in solution to copper. This indicates that as a Daniell cell is used,

the concentration of the zinc sulphate electrolyte will increase, and the concentration of the copper sulphate electrolyte will decrease.

What happens to electrode potentials if the concentrations of the electrolytes change? Would the Daniell cell continue to have a voltage of 1.10 V? Would it increase or decrease, and by how much? It would be useful to use chemical theory to make accurate predictions. However, there is no substitute for valid and reliable experimental results. Theories are only useful if they fit the data. Examine *table 2.3*. It provides such data. What does it tell you about the electrode of the $Ag(s)/Ag^+(aq)$ cell as the concentration of silver ions decreases?

SAQ 2.14

What would be the electrode potential be at 298 K for a silver ion concentration of $0.0001\,mol\,dm^{-3}$?

The electrode potential falls quite predictably. In any half-cell, the electrode potential is determined by a formula called the Nernst equation:

$$E = E^{\ominus} + \frac{RT}{zF}\ln[A]$$

Where $E^{\ominus}$ is the standard electrode potential, $\frac{R}{F}$ is a constant, T is the temperature, z is the charge on the ion in the half-cell and $[A]$ is the concentration of the ion. You do not need to use this equation in this module, but you should appreciate the general behaviour: for positive ions, z is positive (for silver, $z = +1$) and so a reduction in concentration leads to the electrode potential becoming more negative; for negative ions, z is negative and so a reduction in concentration leads

Concentration of silver ions $[Ag^+(aq)]$ / $mol\,dm^{-3}$	Electrode potential at 298 K / V
5	0.84
2	0.82
1	0.80
0.1	0.74
0.01	0.68
0.001	0.62

● **Table 2.3** The variation of electrode potential for the $Ag(s)/Ag^+(aq)$ cell with the concentration of silver ions

to the electrode potential becoming more positive. If the concentrations are increased, the effects are reversed.

We will consider in more detail the nature of chemical equilibrium in chapter 4 – something we took a brief look at right at the beginning of this chapter.

You have just completed a fairly difficult part of the subject. You have seen simple definitions developed to cope with more complicated scenarios, and encountered chemistry in which electron flow is promoted by chemical change – or vice versa. Such changes are everywhere around us, in corroding metals, electrical batteries and the metals industry. We understand enough about them to make predictions. What voltage will a cell have? Will a reaction 'go'? What could reduce an ore of gold to the precious metal itself? Examples of some electrochemical reactions and their relevance to the world we live in can be seen in the end-of-chapter questions.

SUMMARY

■ Redox reactions are reactions in which one (or more) of the reactants is *red*uced and one (or more) of the reactants is *ox*idised. Reduction and oxidation go hand-in-hand: if a reactant is reduced then another reactant must be oxidised, and vice versa.

■ Reduction is a gain of electrons; the oxidation number of the reduced reactant is correspondingly decreased. Oxidation is a loss of electrons; the oxidation number of the oxidised reactant is correspondingly increased.

■ The standard electrode potential, $E^\ominus(298)$, of a half-cell (for example a metal in contact with a solution of its ions) is the voltage measured when the half-cell is connected to form a circuit with a standard hydrogen electrode. The concentration(s) of the solution(s) must be $1.0\,mol\,dm^{-3}$ and the standard conditions of pressure ($101\,kPa$) and temperature ($298\,K$) must apply.

■ The standard hydrogen electrode consists of a platinum plate in contact with a $1.0\,mol\,dm^{-3}$ solution of hydrogen ions.

■ A standard cell potential, $E^\ominus(298)_{cell}$, is the combination of two standard electrode potentials. If the combination of the two half-cells is written like this:

   more negative half-cell ¦¦ more positive half-cell

then

   $E^\ominus(298)_{cell} = E^\ominus(298)_{right} - E^\ominus(298)_{left}$

■ If we bear in mind that the more positive half-cell is written on the right, then the full cell statement is written like this:

| reduced species | oxidised species | oxidised species | reduced species |

■ The electron flow in a cell is from left to right in the cell statement, that is from the more negative half-cell to the more positive half-cell.

■ Cell potentials may be used to see if reactions are feasible. If the cell potential of a reaction is positive, then that reaction *may* be possible. If the cell potential is negative, then the reaction is impossible.

■ Half-cell equations can be combined to form full reaction equations. In doing this, the numbers of electrons exchanged between the half-cells must be balanced.

■ Electrode potentials vary with the concentrations of the aqueous ions. For positive ions, a reduction in the concentration leads to the electrode potential becoming more negative. For negative ions, a reduction in the concentration leads to the electrode potential becoming more positive. These effects are reversed for increases in concentration.

Q*uestions*

1 Use the oxidation number rules to work out the oxidation numbers of each element in the following species:

NaCl   NaOH CH_4 K_2SO_4
NH_4NO_3 CH_3OH

In the following reactions, what is oxidised and what is reduced?

a $H_2O(g) + C(s) \xrightarrow{\text{heat}} H_2(g) + CO(g);$
$(\Delta H$ is negative)

b $Cu(s) + 2H_2SO_4(l) \xrightarrow{\text{heat}} CuSO_4(aq)$
$+ 2H_2O(l) + SO_2(g)$

c $Pb(NO_3)_2(aq) + 2KI(aq)$
$\longrightarrow PbI_2(s) + 2KNO_3(aq)$

2 Particles of gold are often too small to be separated from waste minerals (gangue) by physical methods such as panning. Dissolving them in mercury (in which the gangue does not dissolve) is a method used by peasant miners in South America, who then boil off the mercury in open pots, leaving a residue of gold behind. Larger mining concerns make use of sodium cyanide solution and zinc as shown in the equations below:

$4Au(s) + 8NaCN(aq)$
$\longrightarrow 8Na^+(aq) + 4e^- + 4[Au(CN)_2]^-(aq)$
(2.8)

$2[Au(CN)_2]^-(aq) + Zn(s)$
$\longrightarrow 2Au(s) + [Zn(CN)_4]^{2-}(aq)$ (2.9)

a In each of the reactions above, state which species have been oxidised and which have been reduced. Justify your decisions in terms of electron transfer.

b Check your decisions using changes in oxidation numbers.

c Identify the environmental hazards that are inherent in both the gold-refining methods described above.

3 Hydrogen sulphide is a contaminant of natural gas. It is removed from natural gas by trapping it in 2-aminoethanol, $HOCH_2CH_2NH_2$, from which it is then separated and reacted with oxygen as shown in the equations below (state symbols omitted):

$2H_2S + O_2 \longrightarrow 2S + 2H_2O$ (2.10)
$2H_2S + 3O_2 \longrightarrow 2SO_2 + 2H_2O$ (2.11)
$2H_2S + SO_2 \longrightarrow 3S + 2H_2O$ (2.12)

a In each of the reactions above, state which species have been oxidised and which have been reduced. Justify your decisions in terms of the redox model that is most appropriate.

b In which ways might hydrogen sulphide be considered a problem if it was not removed from natural gas?

4 Using the data in *table 2.1* (page 30), predict what (if anything) would happen if:

a magnesium ribbon was put into silver nitrate solution;

b a silver spoon was left in sodium chloride solution;

c the layer of zinc covering the mild steel of a wheel-barrow was damaged so that air and water could reach both metals;

d the layer of tin covering the mild steel of a baked bean can was damaged so that air and water could reach both metals.

5 Write equations for the reactions that would occur if the following half-cells were connected:

a $F_2(aq)/2F^-(aq)$ and $MnO_4^-(aq)/Mn^{2+}(aq)$

b $Cl_2(aq)/2Cl^-(aq)$ and $MnO_4^-(aq)/Mn^{2+}(aq)$
(Use the value $E^\ominus(298)_{Cl_2/Cl^-} = +1.36\,V$.)

Chemical kinetics

1 understand and use the terms *rate of a reaction*, *rate equation*, *order of a reaction*, *rate constant*, *half-life*, *rate-determining step*, *activation energy* and *catalysis*;

2 construct and use rate equations;

3 deduce the order of a reaction by the initial-rates method and by using concentration–time graphs;

4 understand the relationship between reaction mechanism and the order of the reaction;

5 calculate an initial rate of a reaction using concentration data;

6 understand that the half-life of a first-order reaction is independent of the concentration, and use this half-life in calculations;

7 calculate a rate constant using the initial-rates method;

8 describe a suitable experiment for studying the rate of a reaction;

9 explain the effect of concentration changes on the rate of a reaction;

10 explain what is meant by the term *activation energy*, with reference to the Boltzmann distribution;

11 explain the effect of temperature change on a rate constant;

12 understand how the presence of a catalyst affects the reaction mechanism, and relate this to changes in the Boltzmann distribution;

13 understand what is meant by the terms *homogeneous* and *heterogeneous* catalysis;

14 describe how enzymes behave as biological catalysts;

15 describe the economic importance of catalysts;

16 understand how catalysts are used in the control of pollution from vehicles, and explain how lead in petrol 'poisons' the catalyst.

Rates and reactions

Racing drivers are interested in rate – how fast a car goes. They need to cover a given distance in the shortest possible time. In the 1994 British Grand Prix, Damon Hill completed the 303.4 kilometre race in 1 hour, 30 minutes and 3.64 seconds. Damon's average rate was 202.1 kilometres per hour, the distance travelled divided by the time taken. During the race, his speed changed moment by moment. There was no on-board speedometer, but timed sections of the course put his speed from around $100\,\mathrm{km\,h^{-1}}$ to $300\,\mathrm{km\,h^{-1}}$.

In chemical kinetics we are also interested in rate – how fast a reaction goes. Before the Second World War, it took about a week to make nitro-glycerine, a high explosive, in commercial quantities. During the War, research by an ICI chemist increased the rate by about seven times – very useful at the time. Not that rate is everything. Chemists have to deliver significant amounts of product as well, to get the yield as high as possible. Sometimes an increased reaction rate can diminish the yield, so a good understanding of how much and how fast is very important.

During chemical changes, amounts of substances change. Some disappear altogether. Others appear as a result of the change. A simple example is shown in *figure 3.1*.

SAQ 3.1

Write the cell statement for the reaction of copper sulphate solution with iron wool and confirm theoretically that the change shown in *figure 3.1* should happen.

The beaker in *figure 3.1a* contains $1\,\mathrm{dm^3}$ of $1.00\,\mathrm{mol\,dm^{-3}}$ aqueous copper sulphate, so it contains one mole of copper ions ($63.5\,\mathrm{g}$ of them). Iron wool reacts with the copper ions in solution, displacing them and changing the colour of the solution as a result.

$$Cu^{2+}(aq) + Fe(s) \longrightarrow Fe^{2+}(aq) + Cu(s)$$

● *Figure 3.1* Copper ions replacing atoms of iron.

You can try this experiment on a smaller scale yourself. *Figure 3.1b* shows the reaction 100 seconds later. During this time, some copper ions have been removed from solution, so the concentration of copper ions is less than it was before. *Figure 3.1c* shows the reaction after it has finished. No copper ions are left in solution.

We can estimate the rate of reaction during the first 100 seconds by watching the colour change. We can observe the reduced blueness of the aqueous copper sulphate with a colorimeter, and we can estimate its concentration after 100 seconds.

Experiment might tell you the concentration of copper ions after 100 s was $0.75 \, \mathrm{mol \, dm^{-3}}$. Since the initial concentration was $1.00 \, \mathrm{mol \, dm^{-3}}$, the change of concentration was $0.25 \, \mathrm{mol \, dm^{-3}}$ per 100 s, or $0.0025 \, \mathrm{mol \, dm^{-3} \, s^{-1}}$.

We define **reaction rate** as the change in concentration of a substance divided by the time taken for that change to take place. The unit will therefore be $\mathrm{mol \, dm^{-3} \, s^{-1}}$. If the substance is a reactant and it is being used up, the rate is defined as negative. It is positive if the substance is a product formed during the reaction. In the example above, the reaction rate of copper ions is therefore $-0.0025 \, \mathrm{mol \, dm^{-3} \, s^{-1}}$. It can be written as:

$$\frac{\text{change in } [Cu^{2+}]}{\text{time taken}} = -0.0025 \ \mathrm{mol \, dm^{-3} \, s^{-1}}$$

where the square brackets, [ ], mean 'concentration of whatever is inside them'.

SAQ 3.2

From the equation of the reaction of copper sulphate and iron, deduce the reaction rate of iron.

Rates of reaction – why bother?

Some chemical reactions need to be fast, for example those which go on inside your body when you take a pain-reliever. Some should be as slow as possible, like the corrosion of iron in machinery *(figure 3.2)*.

Biodegradable plastics are used to make shopping bags. Knowing their rate of biodegradation is important. If they biodegrade too quickly, you won't get your shopping home!

The destruction of the ozone layer around the Earth is another example of the importance of reaction rate – we must find ways to slow the rate of ozone destruction.

● *Figure 3.2* Rate is important.

Measuring rates of reaction

How can we measure the rates at which reactions occur? In theory this is quite simple, although in practice great difficulties can arise. The first thing to do is to analyse the reaction, to establish the stoichiometry of the reaction. In other words we need to know how much of each reagent and product is involved.

This sounds pretty obvious, but it is surprising how often this elementary consideration is forgotten, even in research laboratories. For example, in the reaction between nitrogen monoxide (NO) and ozone (O_3), it is necessary to establish that no other products are formed. If there were, our measurements and calculations might not be accurate.

Once the stoichiometry of the reaction is known, and the equation written, we can look for the best ways of measuring rates of change. This could mean measuring amounts of product formed or reagents used. We could make use of colour changes, electrical conductivity changes, pressure changes – whatever is most convenient.

Using colour intensity to monitor change of concentration

Figure 3.3 shows three glasses of Ribena diluted with water. Can you tell in which glass the concentration is greatest? Could you rank them in order of concentration? Could you tell how much Ribena is in each glass?

The answer to the first two questions should be 'yes'. The answer to the third cannot be found without getting an idea of what the colour actually means in terms of concentration.

● **Figure 3.3** Ribena drinks of different concentrations.

● **Figure 3.4** 'Standard' Ribena solutions with an unknown alongside. Try to estimate the concentration of the unknown.

It would be possible to hazard a good guess. You could prepare calibration solutions like these:

a $2.0\,cm^3$ Ribena in $10\,cm^3$ solution
b $1.6\,cm^3$ Ribena in $10\,cm^3$ solution
c $1.2\,cm^3$ Ribena in $10\,cm^3$ solution
d $0.8\,cm^3$ Ribena in $10\,cm^3$ solution
e $0.4\,cm^3$ Ribena in $10\,cm^3$ solution

You could put them in specimen tubes like the ones shown in *figure 3.4*. They must all be filled to the same level.

You could take a sample of Ribena from one of the glasses and put it into an identical tube, to exactly the same depth. It may be better to look down from above to distinguish the colours. This increases the amount of liquid that the light passes through, so that faint colours show up better. It also helps to standardise how far away from the samples your eyes are.

This method could be used to estimate the concentration of copper ions in the experiment on page 39. You could have a range of coloured solutions, each representing a concentration from (say) 1 to $0.1\,mol\,dm^{-3}$. There might be better methods of course, and scientists spend much of their time inventing improved methods and equipment. For example, a simple colorimeter for measuring the concentration of chlorine is shown in *figure 3.5*.

A spectrophotometer is often used to measure colour concentration. The word 'spectrophotometer' means 'light-measurer making use of part of the spectrum'. In practice the spectrophotometer measures how much light of a particular wavelength can pass through a sample, liquid or gas.

● *Figure 3.5* A colorimeter is used to analyse the concentration of chlorine in drinking water.

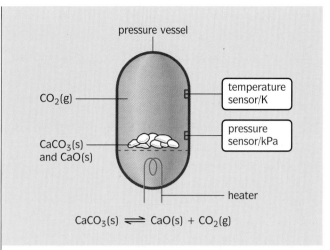

$$CaCO_3(s) \rightleftharpoons CaO(s) + CO_2(g)$$

● *Figure 3.6* A notional system to investigate the effect of heat on the decomposition of limestone.

Monitoring reaction rates of gases using pressure changes

Measurements of pressure change at a given temperature can be used to calculate concentration change as a reaction proceeds. For example, this method can be used to monitor the production of carbon dioxide from limestone in a sealed container *(figure 3.6)*.

Monitoring reaction rates of solutions using chemical analysis

If there is a change in acidity or basicity as a reaction proceeds, suitable titrations can be made to follow the rate. The rate of formation of sulphurous acid, H_2SO_3 (a component of acid rain formed by the reaction of sulphur dioxide with water), is followed by measuring the increase in concentration of hydrogen ions produced. This is monitored by titrating samples of the increasingly acidic solution against a basic solution of known concentration, for example $0.001 \, mol \, dm^{-3}$ aqueous sodium hydroxide.

As we go on to study individual cases, we will indicate how the reaction rate might have been measured.

The rate law and the order of reaction

Consider the high temperature conversion of cyclopropane to propene:

$$\underset{H_2C - CH_2}{\overset{CH_2}{\diagup \diagdown}}(g) \longrightarrow CH_3CH = CH_2(g)$$

The reaction is a hydrocarbon isomerisation, in which the new hydrocarbon is an isomer of the original one. *Table 3.1* gives the variation of concentration of propene with time at a temperature of 500 °C. We can define the rate of reaction as follows:

$$\text{rate} = -\frac{d}{dt}[\text{cyclopropane}] = +\frac{d}{dt}[\text{propene}]$$

This states that the rate of decay of cyclopropane equals the rate of production of propene. (The symbol $\frac{d}{dt}$ means 'rate of change of'.) Why is this a valid rate statement for this reaction?

The graph in *figure 3.7* shows the way in which concentration of the reactant and product vary with

Time/min	0	5	10	15	20	25	30	35	40
[cyclopropane]/mol dm⁻³	1.50	1.23	1.00	0.82	0.67	0.55	0.45	0.37	0.33
[propene]/mol dm⁻³	0.00	0.27	0.49	0.68	0.83	0.95	1.08	1.13	1.20

● *Table 3.1* Concentrations of reactant (cyclopropane) and product (propene) at 5 min intervals (temperature = 500 °C (773 K))

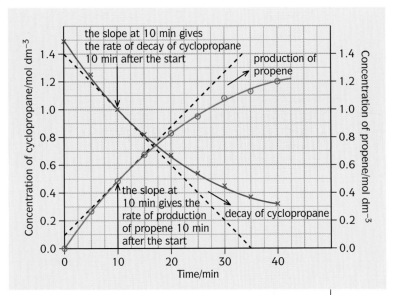

● **Figure 3.7** The decrease in cyclopropane concentration, and the increase in concentration of propene, as the reaction proceeds. Tangents to each curve are drawn at the 10 minute point. Try to relate the figures in the text to this graph.

time. We can use the graph to check the statement

$$-\frac{d}{dt}[\text{cyclopropane}] = +\frac{d}{dt}[\text{propene}]$$

For example, tangents can be drawn to each curve at the 10 min point, as shown in *figure 3.7*. The slope of the line shows the rate of reaction for each substance.

Calculating the rates of reaction 10 min after the start:

$$\begin{aligned}
\text{slope of tangent} \atop \text{for cyclopropane} &= \frac{-1.44\,\text{mol dm}^{-3}}{35 \times 60\,\text{s}} \\
&= -6.7 \times 10^{-4}\,\text{mol dm}^{-3}\text{s}^{-1}
\end{aligned}$$

$$\begin{aligned}
\text{slope of tangent} \atop \text{for propene} &= \frac{(1.29 - 0.08)\,\text{mol dm}^{-3}}{30 \times 60\,\text{s}} \\
&= \frac{1.21\,\text{mol dm}^{-3}}{1800\,\text{s}} \\
&= 6.7 \times 10^{-4}\,\text{mol dm}^{-3}\text{s}^{-1}
\end{aligned}$$

These figures confirm the statement that the rate of production of propene is the same as the rate of decay of cyclopropane at a given time. You could check its accuracy at other points on the graph, for instance after 20 min. Drawing tangents by eye can be very inaccurate, so you can only verify the rate statement approximately.

One factor that influences the rate of a reaction is the temperature. The higher the temperature of the reaction vessel and its contents, the faster the reaction will go. We shall explore this in some detail later. We can easily eliminate this influence by conducting the reaction at a fixed temperature. You will notice therefore that we carefully specify the temperature at which the cyclopropane–propene conversion is carried out. At a different temperature the rate of the reaction would be quite different, and so it is essential in all cases to quote the temperature at which reaction rates have been measured.

The first influence on reaction rate that we shall consider in detail is the concentration of reactant. Take another look at *figure 3.7*. Notice that, as time passes, the concentration of cyclopropane falls – hardly surprising. The question to ask is: 'In what way does it fall?' Does it fall in a predictable way? Is there a mathematical way of describing it?

Figure 3.8 supplies some answers. We will use it to calculate the rate of reaction at different concentrations: $1.5\,\text{mol dm}^{-3}$, $1.0\,\text{mol dm}^{-3}$, and $0.5\,\text{mol dm}^{-3}$. (Again, we can measure the rate at any point on a graph by drawing the tangent to the curve and measuring its slope at that point.)

The three measurements are shown in *table 3.2* and are represented by the graph in *figure 3.9*.

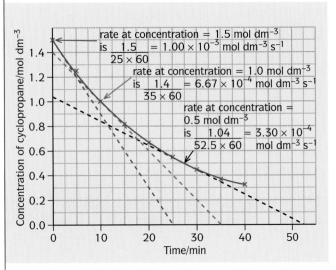

● **Figure 3.8** Calculations of the rate of decay of cyclopropane, made at regular intervals.

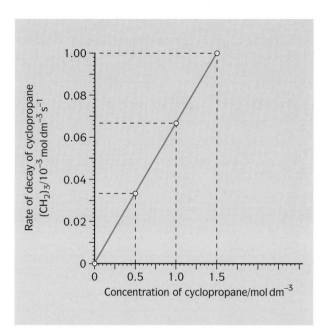

● **Figure 3.9** The rate of decay of cyclopropane. Note how the gradient (rate/concentration) is constant.

The data and the graph show that the rate of the reaction does depend directly upon the concentration of cyclopropane as we predicted. If the concentration of cyclopropene drops to two thirds, so does its reaction rate.

SAQ 3.3

What would be the reaction rate if the concentration of cyclopropane was halved?

The third line in *table 3.2* shows that rate/concentration is a number that is pretty well constant $(0.67 \times 10^{-3}\,s^{-1})$. This can be expressed mathematically:

$$rate = k \times [cyclopropane]$$

The proportionality constant, k, is called the **rate constant**. For the reaction above, it has the units of rate divided by concentration, s^{-1}. For the data of *table 3.2* the rate constant is $6.7 \times 10^{-4}\,s^{-1}$. Drawing tangents by eye is extremely inaccurate and

we can therefore verify our statement only approximately. Accurate mathematical procedures involving integral calculus show that it is obeyed exactly.

Rate equations

We already have a rate equation for the decomposition of cyclopropane:

$$rate = k\,[cyclopropane]$$

It was found by experiment – not by theoretical calculation.

The reaction between hydrogen gas and nitrogen monoxide, NO, at $800\,°C$ produces water and nitrogen gas:

$$2H_2(g) + 2NO(g) \longrightarrow 2H_2O(g) + N_2(g)$$

Experiment shows that doubling the concentration of hydrogen doubles the reaction rate, tripling $[H_2]$ triples the rate, and so on. So

$$rate \propto [H_2] \qquad or \qquad rate = k_1 \times [H_2]$$

Further experiment shows that doubling the concentration of nitrogen monoxide quadruples the reaction rate (2^2), tripling $[NO]$ increases it by a factor of nine (3^2), and so on. Therefore

$$rate \propto [NO]^2 \qquad or \qquad rate = k_2 \times [NO]^2$$

The two equations can be combined as follows:

$$rate \propto [H_2][NO]^2$$
$$or \qquad rate = k_1 \times k_2 \times [H_2] \times [NO]^2$$
$$= k \times [H_2] \times [NO]^2$$

(where $k_1 \times k_2 = k$), which can be written as

$$rate = k[H_2][NO]^2$$

More rate equations are shown in *table 3.3*. They were all found by experiment. They cannot be predicted from the equation – so don't assume they can. The units for k may be different for each reaction; they must be worked out for each reaction. For example:

$$k[H_2][NO]^2 = rate\ in\ mol\,dm^{-3}\,s^{-1}$$

so k is in $\dfrac{(mol\,dm^{-3}\,s^{-1})}{(mol\,dm^{-3}) \times (mol\,dm^{-3})^2}$

i.e. k's units are $mol^{-2}\,dm^6\,s^{-1}$.

concentration/mol dm^{-3}	1.5	1.0	0.5
rate/mol dm^{-3} s^{-1}	1.00×10^{-3}	6.67×10^{-4}	3.30×10^{-4}
$\dfrac{rate}{concentration}$ / s^{-1}	0.67×10^{-3}	0.67×10^{-3}	0.66×10^{-3}

● **Table 3.2** Rates of decay for cyclopropane at different concentrations, calculated from *figure 3.8*

Equation for the reaction	Rate equation	Units for k
$2H_2(g) + 2NO(g) \longrightarrow 2H_2O(g) + N_2(g)$	rate = $k[H_2][NO]^2$	$mol^{-2}\,dm^6\,s^{-1}$
$H_2(g) + I_2(g) \longrightarrow 2HI(g)$	rate = $k[H_2][I_2]$	$mol^{-1}\,dm^3\,s^{-1}$
$NO(g) + CO(g) + O_2(g) \longrightarrow NO_2(g) + CO_2(g)$	rate = $k[NO]^2$	$mol^{-1}\,dm^3\,s^{-1}$

● **Table 3.3** Rate equations for some reactions

Order of reaction

The order of a reaction gives us an idea of how the concentration of a reagent affects the reaction rate. It is defined as follows: the **order of a reaction** is the power to which we have to raise the concentration to fit the rate equation.

The easiest way to explain order is to use an example.

■ Chemical equation:
$$2NO(g) + O_2(g) \longrightarrow 2NO_2(g)$$
■ Experimental rate equation:
rate = $k[NO]^2[O_2]^1 = k[NO]^2[O_2]$

The order of the reaction as far as nitrogen monoxide (NO) is concerned is 2. It is the power of 2 in $[NO]^2$. We say the reaction is 'second order with respect to nitrogen monoxide'.

The order of reaction as far as oxygen is concerned is 1. We say the reaction is 'first order with respect to oxygen'.

Overall, the order of reaction is 2 + 1 = 3. Note how careful you should be when you talk about reaction orders. Always ask yourself the question: 'Order with respect to *what*?'

SAQ 3.4

What is the order of reaction for the decompositon of cyclopropane to propene? The rate equation is

rate = k[cyclopropane]

Zeroth-order reactions

Ammonia gas decomposes on a hot tungsten wire.

$$2NH_3(g) \overset{W}{\longrightarrow} N_2(g) + 3H_2(g)$$

The rate of decomposition, $\frac{d}{dt}[NH_3]$, does not depend upon the concentration of ammonia gas. The rate of reaction is fixed. Doubling and tripling the concentration of ammonia makes no difference to the rate at which the ammonia decomposes. Thus

$$-\frac{d}{dt}[NH_3] = k$$

which can be written as

$$-\frac{d}{dt}[NH_3] = k[NH_3]^0$$

(since anything to the power 0 equals 1). This can be represented on a graph as shown in *figure 3.10*.

First-order reactions

The gas dinitrogen oxide, N_2O, decomposes on a heated gold surface:

$$2N_2O(g) \overset{Au}{\longrightarrow} 2N_2(g) + O_2(g)$$

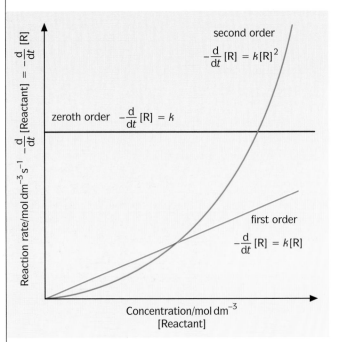

● **Figure 3.10** Zeroth-, first- and second-order reactions: how changes in the concentration of a reactant affect the reaction rate.

The rate of decomposition, $\frac{d}{dt}[N_2O]$, depends directly upon the concentration of N_2O. If its concentration is doubled, its reaction rate doubles. Thus

$$-\frac{d}{dt}[N_2O] = k[N_2O]$$

which can be written as

$$-\frac{d}{dt}[N_2O] = k[N_2O]^1$$

(since anything to the power 1 is unchanged). This can be represented on a graph as shown in *figure 3.10*.

Second-order reactions

Ethanal vapour (CH_3CHO) decomposes at $800\,K$:

$$CH_3CHO(g) \longrightarrow CH_4(g) + CO(g)$$

The rate of decomposition, $\frac{d}{dt}[CH_3CHO]$, depends directly upon the square of the concentration of CH_3CHO. If its concentration is doubled, its reaction rate quadruples. Thus

$$-\frac{d}{dt}[CH_3CHO] = k[CH_3CHO]^2$$

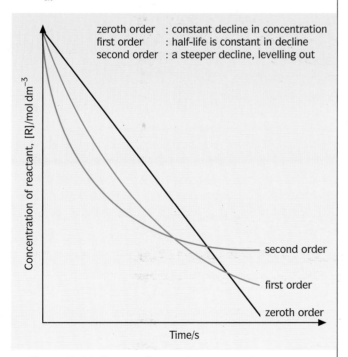

zeroth order : constant decline in concentration
first order : half-life is constant in decline
second order : a steeper decline, levelling out

● **Figure 3.11** Zeroth-, first- and second-order reactions: how changes in the concentration of a reactant affect the time taken for a reaction to proceed.

This can be represented on a graph as shown in *figure 3.10*.

An alternative method of distinguishing between these three types is shown in *figure 3.11*.

Half-life, $t_{1/2}$, and reaction rates

In chemical reactions 'half-life' refers to concentrations of a reactant – it is the time taken for the concentration of a reagent to fall to half its original value.

SAQ 3.5

Use the graph in *figure 3.12* to find the half-life for the thermal decomposition of cyclopropane at $500\,°C$. Is this the same half-life as in *figure 3.8* (page 42), which shows the measurements from the same chemical reaction in a different experiment?

It can be shown mathematically that the half-life of a first order reaction, $t_{1/2}$, is given by $(\ln 2)/k$, which is $0.693/k$. In the case of cyclopropane,

$$t_{1/2} = \frac{0.693}{6.7 \times 10^{-4}\,s^{-1}} = 1034\,s = 17.2\,min$$

As you see from *SAQ 3.5*, your graph enables you to check this value.

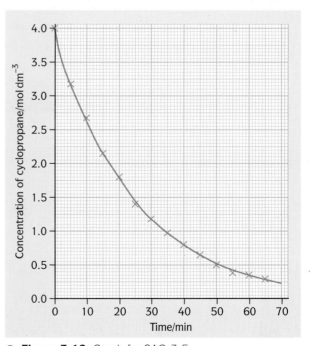

● **Figure 3.12** Graph for *SAQ 3.5*.

Finding the order of reaction using raw data

We are now going to proceed to a more complex example. Keep clear in your mind the meanings of the terms 'reaction rate', 'rate constant', and 'order of reaction'. It helps also to keep tabs on the units you will use.

Table 3.4 gives rate and concentration data for the reaction of methanol with aqueous hydrochloric acid to give chloromethane and water at 298 K:

$$CH_3OH(aq) + HCl(aq) \longrightarrow CH_3Cl(aq) + H_2O(l)$$

Time/min	[HCl]/mol dm^{-3}	[CH$_3$OH]/mol dm^{-3}
0	1.84	1.84
200	1.45	1.45
400	1.22	1.22
600	1.04	1.04
800	0.91	0.91
1000	0.81	0.81
1200	0.72	0.72
1400	0.66	0.66
1600	0.60	0.60
1800	0.56	0.56
2000	0.54	0.54

● **Table 3.4** Data for reaction between methanol and hydrochloric acid

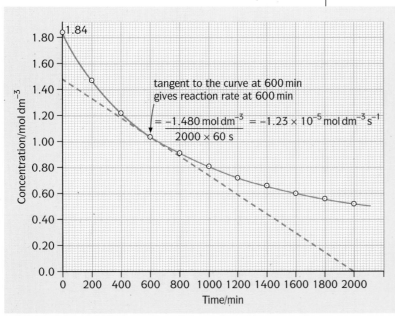

● **Figure 3.13** The concentrations of hydrochloric acid and methanol reduce at the same rate as time elapses.

SAQ 3.6

The data in *table 3.4* could have been obtained by titrating small samples of the reaction mixture with a standard strong base. What would have been found like this? How else might the reaction have been monitored?

Figure 3.13 shows a graph of these data, and the beginnings of an exploration of the data.

First look to see if there is a consistent half-life for this reaction. Half of the initial amount of each reagent is 1.84/2 mol dm^{-3} = 0.92 mol dm^{-3}. The half-life is 780 min. However, this amount, 0.92 mol dm^{-3}, does not halve again in another 780 min. The half-life is not consistent – so the overall order of reaction is not equal to 1.

As with the previous reaction, we can draw tangents to the curve to derive approximate rates at different times. This is shown for $t = 600$ min in *figure 3.13*. Other values have been calculated from this data and are shown in *table 3.5*. You can draw your own graph using the data in *table 3.4* to find out what results *you* obtain – they should vary a bit owing to the difficulty of drawing an accurate tangent by eye.

By examining the data in *table 3.5* you can see that the reaction rate diminishes with time – unlike a zeroth-order reaction. If you plot a graph you will see that it most closely resembles a second-order plot (see *figure 3.10*, page 44). Let's assume that the reaction rate is proportional to the concentration of each of the reagents like this:

$$\text{rate} = k \times [HCl]^1[CH_3OH]^1 \quad (3.1)$$

Rearranging the equation we have

$$K = \frac{\text{rate}}{[HCl][CH_3OH]}$$

We can now substitute values for rate and concentration at any particular time to find out if the calculated value of k is indeed constant. Thus at $t = 600$ min

$$k = \frac{1.23 \times 10^{-5} \text{ mol dm}^{-3}\text{s}^{-1}}{1.04 \text{ mol dm}^{-3} \times 1.04 \text{ mol dm}^{-3}}$$

$$= 1.14 \times 10^{-5} \text{ mol}^{-1} \text{dm}^3 \text{s}^{-1}$$

Time/min	Concentration/mol dm^{-3}	Rate from graph/mol dm^{-3}min^{-1}	Rate from graph/mol dm^{-3}s^{-1}
0	1.84	2.30×10^{-3}	3.83×10^{-5}
200	1.45	1.46×10^{-3}	2.43×10^{-5}
400	1.22	1.05×10^{-3}	1.75×10^{-5}
600	1.04	0.74×10^{-3}	1.23×10^{-5}
800	0.91	0.54×10^{-3}	0.90×10^{-5}

● **Table 3.5** Values calculated for the reaction between methanol and hydrochloric acid

The results in *table 3.6* show that over a range of times during the reaction, *k* is constant. (Although the figures are not exactly equal, they are fairly close considering that tangents were estimated from a graph.)

Table 3.6 shows that the rate law given in *equation 3.1* is followed. This is referred to as a second-order equation, because the sum of the powers to which the individual concentrations are raised in the rate equation is 2. We can say that the reaction is first order in methanol, first order in hydrochloric acid, and second order overall. Notice also that our units for a second-order rate constant are different. Try to confirm that they are correct by examining the units in the calculation for *k*.

In general therefore, suppose we have a reaction between components A, B and C that yields the rate law

rate = $k[A]^x[B]^y[C]^z$

We can say that *x* is the order with respect to A, *y* is the order with respect to B, and *z* is the order with respect to C. The order is *x* + *y* + *z* overall.

The initial-rates method

We have seen that the rate of a reaction changes as the reactants are used up. For some reactions, measuring these changes over time may not be the best method for determining the rate equation. For instance, if the rate is quite slow, then obtaining a useful set of measurements would take an inconvenient amount of time. However, we usually know the initial concentrations of the reactants that we mix together in the reaction flask, and we can measure the initial rate of reaction. (For example, look again at the graph in *figure 3.8*, page 42: the rate we calculated at the concentration of 1.5 mol dm^{-3} is the initial rate.) If we carry out several experiments with different concentrations of reactants, and we measure the initial rates of these experiments, then we can determine the rate equation. The best way to illustrate this is with an example.

Dinitrogen pentaoxide decomposes to nitrogen dioxide and oxygen:

$$2N_2O_5(g) \longrightarrow 4NO_2(g) + O_2(g)$$

Table 3.7 gives the values of the initial rate as it varies with the concentration of dinitrogen pentaoxide. A graph of the data, *figure 3.14*, shows that the initial rate of reaction is directly proportional to the initial concentration:

Rate $\propto [N_2O_5]$
$= k[N_2O_5]$
where $k = 1.05 \times 10^{-5}s^{-1}$.

SAQ 3.7

What is the order of reaction for the decomposition of dinitrogen pentaoxide?

Time/min	Rate constant k /10^{-5}mol^{-1}dm^{3}s^{-1}
0	1.13
200	1.16
400	1.18
600	1.14
800	1.09

● **Table 3.6** Calculations for rate constant *k* assuming that the reaction is first-order with respect to each of the starting reagents

Initial concentration [N$_2$O$_5$]/mol dm^{-3}	Initial rate/mol dm^{-3}s^{-1}
3.00	3.15×10^{-5}
2.51	2.64×10^{-5}
1.12	1.18×10^{-5}
0.50	0.53×10^{-5}

● **Table 3.7** Data for decomposition of dinitrogen pentaoxide

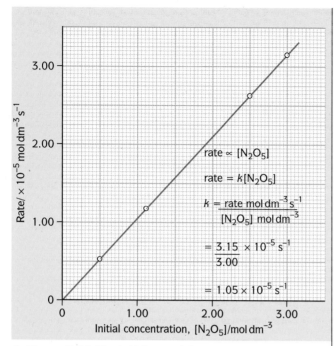

● **Figure 3.14** The initial rate of decomposition of dinitrogen pentaoxide is directly proportional to the initial concentration.

We will now consider a more general example. Chemicals A and B react to produce a third chemical C:

$$3A + 2B \longrightarrow 2C$$

We have the data in *table 3.8* from experiments carried out to measure the initial rates of reaction. (There may be some experimental error.) Note that we have kept the initial concentration of one reactant fixed whilst we have varied the initial concentration of the other reactant.

Consider experiments 1–3: [A] is fixed and [B] is varied. When [B] is doubled, the initial rate doubles (approximately). When [B] is tripled, the initial rate triples. So the rate is proportional to $[B]^1$. Hence we can say that the order of reaction with respect to B is 1.

Now consider experiments 3–5: [B] is fixed and [A] is varied. When [A] is doubled, the initial rate increases by a factor of 4. When [A] is tripled, the initial rate increases by a factor of 9. So the rate is proportional to $[A]^2$. Hence the order of reaction with respect to A is 2.

This gives us a rate equation like this:

$$\text{rate} = k[A]^2[B]^1$$

So the overall order of reaction is 3.

We can also determine the rate constant from the data in *table 3.8*. If we plot initial rate against the concentration of B, using experiments 1–3, we get a straight line (*figure 3.15*). The gradient of this line must be $k \times [A]^2$, because [A] is fixed. So

$$k = \frac{\text{gradient}}{[A]^2} = \frac{[(0.03-0.00)/(0.3-0.0)]\text{s}^{-1}}{(0.10 \text{ mol dm}^{-3})^2}$$

$$= 10 \text{ mol}^{-2} \text{ dm}^6 \text{ s}^{-1}$$

From the above examples we can make some important deductions about the kinetics of chemical processes. As we stressed earlier, the first step in a

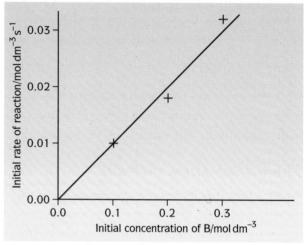

● **Figure 3.15** Initial rate against the concentration of B gives a straight line.

Experiment	*Initial concentration of A*/mol dm^{-3}	*Initial concentration of B*/mol dm^{-3}	*Initial rate of reaction*/mol dm^{-3} s^{-1}
1	0.10	0.10	0.010
2	0.10	0.20	0.019
3	0.10	0.30	0.032
4	0.20	0.30	0.12
5	0.30	0.30	0.28

● **Table 3.8** Initial rates of reactions between A and B

kinetic investigation is to establish the stoichiometry of the reaction, so we must analyse all the reaction products. This enables us to write the chemical equation. However, there is no correspondence between the stoichiometric equation for the reaction and the rate equation. We certainly cannot predict one from the other.

Rate equations – the pay-off

Chemists are particularly interested in the mechanisms of chemical reactions – which chemical bonds are broken, which are made and in what order. By using the rate equation, sometimes along with other items of information, we can deduce something about the separate bond-making and bond-breaking processes that go to make up the overall reaction.

Some reactions may consist of a single step. For example, when aqueous sodium hydroxide is mixed with dilute hydrochloric acid, the reaction is simply one in which hydrogen ions pair up with hydroxide ions to form water. The other ions do not participate in the reaction – they just get left alongside each other in solution:

$$Na^+(aq) + OH^-(aq) + H^+(aq) + Cl^-(aq)$$
$$\longrightarrow H_2O(l) + Na^+(aq) + Cl^-(aq)$$

Very frequently, a reaction is made up of a number of sequential steps. Each step will have a rate associated with it, but to find the overall rate of reaction, all we need to know is the rate of the *slowest* step (also called the **rate-determining step**). This is the case when all other steps are much faster. Fast steps, like selecting items off shelves in a supermarket, become insignificant when compared to the slow step, like queuing at the checkout.

We use the following principle, by which we can use the rate equation to construct the reaction mechanism: *If the concentration of a reactant appears in the rate equation, then that reactant or something derived from it takes part in the slow step of the reaction. If it does not appear in the rate equation, then neither the reactant nor anything derived from it participates in the slow step.*

This is the key to the interpretation of rate equations in terms of mechanisms of reactions. We can now consider some of the reactions we have looked at above, in terms of what their kinetic character, and other data, may tell us of their mechanism.

Reaction mechanisms

We look again at the reaction for the decomposition of dinitrogen pentaoxide:

$$2N_2O_5(g) \longrightarrow 4NO_2(g) + O_2(g)$$

You may have been surprised that this did not turn out to be a second-order reaction. The stoichiometry is bimolecular – we need two molecules of dinitrogen pentaoxide to balance the equation. So we can imagine that the reaction *might* start by two N_2O_5 molecules colliding and breaking up as suggested in the equation shown in *figure 3.16*.

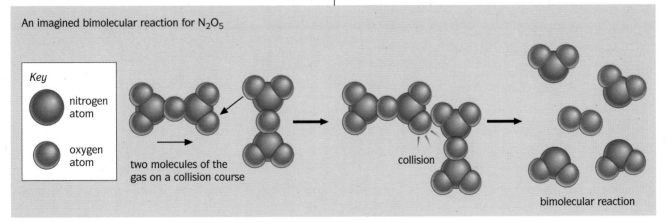

An imagined bimolecular reaction for N_2O_5

Key

nitrogen atom

oxygen atom

two molecules of the gas on a collision course

collision

bimolecular reaction

● **Figure 3.16** The equation for the decomposition of dinitrogen pentaoxide suggests that a reaction between two molecules occurs (a bimolecular reaction). The rate equation tells us otherwise.

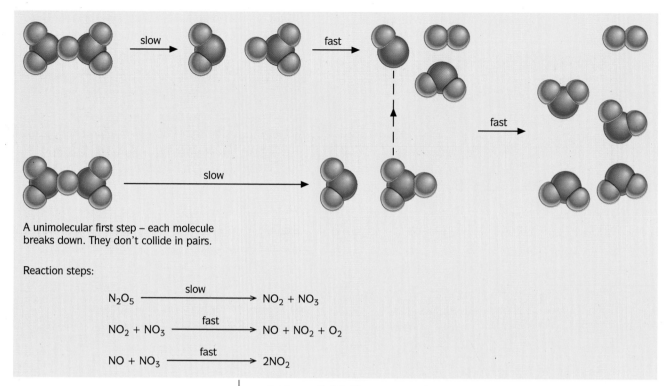

A unimolecular first step – each molecule breaks down. They don't collide in pairs.

Reaction steps:

$$N_2O_5 \xrightarrow{\text{slow}} NO_2 + NO_3$$

$$NO_2 + NO_3 \xrightarrow{\text{fast}} NO + NO_2 + O_2$$

$$NO + NO_3 \xrightarrow{\text{fast}} 2NO_2$$

● **Figure 3.17** The rate equation tells us that the decomposition of individual molecules of dinitrogen pentaoxide is the rate-determining step. The subsequent reactions are much faster by comparison, and do not have much influence on the overall rate. Try to match the equations with the illustrations to get a picture of what is happening.

But the rate equation tells us something different.

$$\text{rate} = k[N_2O_5]$$

The rate equation tells us that the slow step of the reaction involves *one* molecule of dinitrogen pentaoxide decomposing (to nitrogen dioxide and nitrogen trioxide). This is the first step. The subsequent steps are comparatively fast. (*Fast* and *slow* are not absolute terms, so when we speak of fast and slow steps within the context of a given reaction, we mean relative to one another.) The actual mechanism of this reaction is shown in *figure 3.17*. The first step of the reaction is the slow step. It is also known as the elementary step, and we notice that for this step the number of molecules reacting in the stoichiometric equation is the same as its order – both are 1.

Now let's look at the acid-catalysed reaction of propanone with iodine:

$$CH_3COCH_3(aq) + I_2(aq) \xrightarrow{H^+(aq)} CH_3COCH_2I(aq) + HI(aq)$$

It appears that hydrogen ions from the acid are not directly involved. Either they are not used up or they are regenerated with the products, at the same rate as they are used up. In either case the hydrogen ions behave as a catalyst.

The rate equation sheds some light on this. (Remember that the rate equation must always be determined by experiment.) It is

$$\text{rate} = k[CH_3COCH_3][H^+] = k[CH_3COCH_3]^1[H^+]^1[I_2]^0$$

Therefore, the rate-determining step must involve propanone and hydrogen ions. Since the concentration of iodine does not occur in the rate equation, then iodine does not participate in the rate determining step – the reaction is zeroth order with respect to iodine, which means that the reaction proceeds until all the iodine is used up (*figure 3.18a*).

The mechanism of the reaction is given in *figure 3.18b*. Notice that the slow step does not involve either propanone or hydrogen ions directly, but *something derived from them both*, protonated

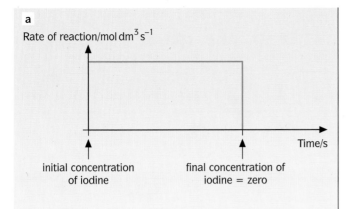

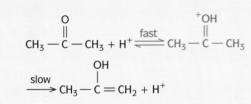

• **Figure 3.18**

a A graph consistent with the zeroth order of reaction for iodine in the acid-catalysed iodination of propanone.

b The slow step is the first step – the reaction of hydrogen ions with propanone molecules.

propanone. Iodine intrudes later in the sequence, in what must be a subsequent fast step. We can picture the reaction sequence as follows. The propanone exists in equilibrium with its protonated form (we shall discuss something more of acid–base equilibria in the next section). Every now and then one of these protonated molecules decomposes to lose H^+, not from the oxygen atom but from carbon, to yield the intermediate $CH_3COH=CH_2$. We could not have deduced this reaction scheme precisely from the rate equation, but it does fit in with that equation. Confirmatory evidence is given by the fact that if we carry out the reaction not with iodine, but with heavy water, D_2O, a deuterium atom, D, (a hydrogen atom with a neutron, as well as a proton, in the

nucleus) is taken up by the methyl group of the propanone at exactly the same rate as iodine is in the first reaction. The two reactions have the same rate-determining steps.

A reaction revisited

The rate equation for the reaction between methanol and hydrochloric acid is established by experiment:

$$CH_3OH(aq) + HCl(aq) \longrightarrow CH_3Cl(aq) + H_2O(l)$$

$$rate = k[CH_3OH][HCl]$$

Extra information can help us to formulate a reaction mechanism. The rate equation suggests that a simple readjustment of bonds in a single-step reaction is involved (*figure 3.19*).

However, experiments show that the rate can be increased by the addition of a strong acid, H^+ ions, to the reaction mixture as well as by the addition of sodium chloride or a similar source of chloride ions, Cl^-. It is clear that the rate equation does not cater for the separate effects of varying concentrations of hydrogen ions and chloride ions. The new rate equation that is correct for hydrochloric acid, but also accounts for the separate effects of hydrogen ions and chloride ions, is:

$$rate = k[CH_3OH][H^+][Cl^-]$$

Now let us re-examine the proposed mechanism for this reaction in the light of the more general rate equation. The first stage consists of a protonation equilibrium:

$$H_3C - OH + H^+ \rightleftharpoons H_3C - \overset{+}{O}\underset{H}{\overset{H}{<}}$$

This is followed by an attack by the chloride ion.

$$H - \overset{\overset{\displaystyle H}{|}}{\underset{\underset{\displaystyle H}{|}}{C}} - O - H \xrightarrow{\text{slow}} H - \overset{\overset{\displaystyle H}{|}}{\underset{\underset{\displaystyle H}{|}}{C}} - Cl + O - H$$
$$Cl - H \qquad\qquad H$$

bonds seem to break...and remake

• **Figure 3.19** An apparent mechanism for the reaction between methanol and hydrochloric acid.

SAQ 3.8

Write the second stage of the reaction between methanol and hydrochloric acid so that it fits the rate equation based upon the supplementary facts we know about the reaction.

The collision theory of reactivity

We have studied in detail how concentration of reactants influences the rate of reaction. The greater the concentration of the reactants in the rate-determining step, the faster the reaction goes. Why should this be? We can get some idea by considering a simple gas-phase reaction between two molecular species A and B to give C and D.

It's not hard to imagine that the reaction between reagents A and B occurs by two molecules of A and B colliding. Not all collisions are

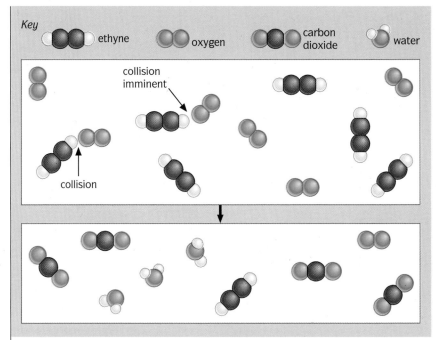

Key: ethyne, oxygen, carbon dioxide, water

collision imminent

collision

● **Figure 3.20** Molecules of ethyne, $C_2H_2(g)$, and oxygen, $O_2(g)$, can collide. If the collision is big enough, chemical bonds are broken. They are re-formed when the fragments combine to make new molecules: carbon dioxide, $CO_2(g)$, and steam, $H_2O(g)$.

effective. A collision is not necessarily followed by a reaction, and we shall explore this possibility later. However, a reaction certainly *cannot* occur if the molecules don't collide. An example well known to engineers is shown in *figures 3.20* and *3.21*.

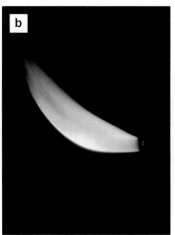

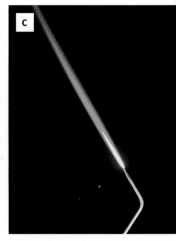

● **Figure 3.21**

a Ethyne is produced by an oxyacetylene torch. Here the gas is not ignited, and you can see it bubbling through water.

b The ethyne is now ignited, but is not completely combusting because the yellow flame indicates the presence of carbon: the temperature of the flame is relatively low.

c The ethyne is now being completely converted into carbon dioxide and water: the temperature of the flame is much higher.

SAQ 3.9

Write the chemical equation for the reaction in *figure 3.20*.

This simple notion is the basis of the collision theory of reactivity. This implies that if there are more molecules of A and B in a given volume (the concentrations of A and B are higher), then the number of collisions increases, and so the reaction proceeds at a faster rate.

SAQ 3.10

Figure 3.22 shows two equal-sized containers of the molecules of A and B, at the same temperature and before they react. In which is the concentration higher? In which will the rate of reaction be greater?

In studying the influence of concentration on rate, we have to be careful to keep temperature constant, because a change in temperature will alter the reaction rate. The qualitative influence is for an increase in temperature to increase reaction rate, and using the simple collision theory model it is not hard to see why. There will be a wide distribution of energies (and therefore speeds) of molecules of A and B, but increasing the temperature will certainly increase the average speed of the molecules. Indeed, an increase in temperature is the same thing as an increase in the random kinetic energies, and hence the speeds, of the molecules. The increased speeds of molecules of A and B will lead to a greater average energy of collision between them, so more molecules will react.

We can summarise all this as follows:

■ Molecules will react only if they collide with each other.
■ Reactions will occur if there is enough energy in the collison.
■ Increased concentration increases the likelihood of collision, which increases reaction rate.
■ Increased temperature increases the average energy of collision, which increases reaction rate.

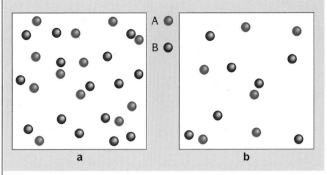

● *Figure 3.22*

The Boltzmann distribution

In any mixture of moving molecules, the energy of each molecule varies enormously. Like bumper cars at a fairground, some are belting along at high speeds while others are virtually at a standstill. The situation changes moment by moment: a car (or particle) travelling at a fairly gentle pace can get a shunt from behind and speed off with much greater energy than before; the fast car (or particle) that caused the collision will slow down during the collision.

The Boltzmann distribution represents the numbers of cars (or particles) with particular energies. It does not work too well for bumper cars, but it does with samples of gas, where there are billions and billions of molecules in constant random motion. A few are almost motionless. A minority have momentary speeds far in excess of the average. The majority have speeds around an average value. This is illustrated by the graph shown in *figure 3.23*.

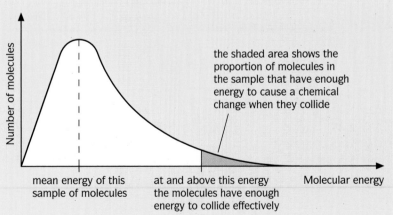

● *Figure 3.23* The Boltzmann distribution for molecular energies in a sample of gas. Since the mass of each molecule is the same, the difference in energies is due to a difference in speed. Note the asymmetric shape of the curve.

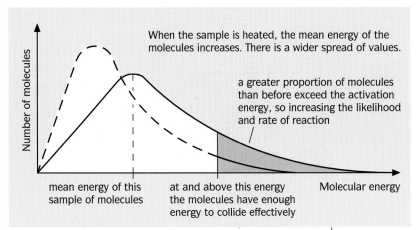

When the sample is heated, the mean energy of the molecules increases. There is a wider spread of values.

a greater proportion of molecules than before exceed the activation energy, so increasing the likelihood and rate of reaction

Number of molecules

mean energy of this sample of molecules

at and above this energy the molecules have enough energy to collide effectively

Molecular energy

● *Figure 3.24* Note how the Boltzmann distribution flattens and shifts to the right at the higher temperature. The areas under both curves are the same – they represent the total number of molecules in the sample, and this should not change before a reaction occurs.

This average value will increase if the temperature of the entire collection of molecules is increased. Some molecules will still be almost immobile, but at any one time there is a greater number at a higher speed than before. The new distribution is shown in *figure 3.24*. The effect of this shift in the distribution is to bring more molecules closer to, or over, the activation energy.

Activation energy

Just as two cars with effective bumpers may collide at low speed with no real damage being done (apart from frayed tempers), so low-energy collisions will not result in reaction. The molecules will bounce apart unchanged (*figure 3.25*). On the other hand, a high speed collision between one car and another will result in permanent damage, and the configuration of each vehicle will be drastically altered (and the same may go for the drivers). In the same sort of way, molecules have to collide with a certain minimum energy E_a for there to be a chance of reaction. E_a is referred to as the **activation energy** for the reaction between A and B, for a mole of such molecules. For the simple reaction we are considering, it is equal to the bond energy of the bonds that are being broken in the reaction.

But why should we have to surmount this energy barrier E_a to bring about reaction? After all, as we saw in chapter 1, if the reaction between A and B is exothermic, the energy of bonds formed in the product molecules is greater than the energy of bonds broken A and B. Why doesn't the reaction flow spontaneously downhill from A and B to give C and D, as illustrated in *figure 3.26*?

Before we consider the answer to this question, it must be pointed out that such a situation could be inconvenient, if not catastrophic. We will consider a simple example to show this. Consider the equation for the combustion of methane (which is in natural gas) and oxygen to give carbon dioxide and water:

$$CH_4(g) + 2O_2(g) \longrightarrow CO_2(g) + 2H_2O(g);$$
$$\Delta H = -1802 \, kJ \, mol^{-1}$$

● *Figure 3.25* These collisions, frequent as they are, are not effective. They do not, we hope, result in permanent damage – chemical change.

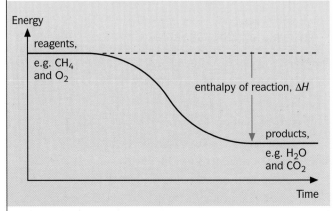

Energy

reagents, e.g. CH_4 and O_2

enthalpy of reaction, ΔH

products, e.g. H_2O and CO_2

Time

● *Figure 3.26* A 'down-hill-all-the-way' reaction. Fortunately, it does not happen for methane and oxygen at normal temperatures and pressures.

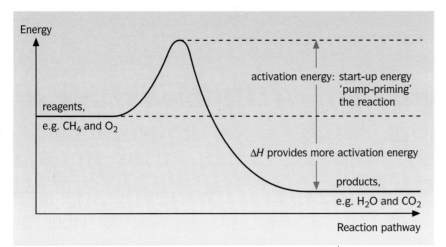

● **Figure 3.27** A reaction pathway diagram, showing the activation energy. This is an exothermic reaction.

We have to ignite the methane; that is, we must give it sufficient energy for the reaction to get started. There is no reaction between the two gases before ignition, and without this boost they sit together quite contentedly for an indefinite length of time. This is due to the fact that, as the methane and oxygen molecules approach one another, the filled electronic levels of one molecule repel the filled electronic levels of the other. It's only if this repulsion can be overcome by a substantial input of energy that the attractive forces (between the electrons of one molecule and the nuclear charge of the other) can take over. The redistribution of electrons that occurs results in the bond-breaking and bond-making processes – it sets off a molecular reaction.

Once the reaction has started, enough heat energy is produced to keep the reaction going (it is **self-sustained**). *Figure 3.27* shows the situation diagrammatically. Overall the reaction pathway (or coordinate) lies downhill, but initially the path lies uphill.

SAQ 3.11
In the case of the reaction between methane and oxygen, where could the activation energy come from?

SAQ 3.12
Examples of ordered instability and disordered stability are shown in *figure 3.29*. Which has the lower entropy? Which has the higher entropy and with it the greater stability?

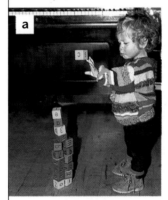

● **Figure 3.29** Entropy at work.

Why should endothermic reactions go at all?

If we have a reaction that is exothermic, it is obvious why the reaction should proceed to give the more stable products, so long as it is provided with a boost to enable it to surmount its particular activation barrier. But why ever should we be able to get an endothermic reaction to go?

Not only do we have the activation barrier to get over, but even when we do this, the energy of the product molecules is greater than the energy of the reactant molecules *(figure 3.28)*. We have an apparent decrease in stability – the reaction has 'gone uphill'. We can only say that this is a very legitimate question to which the answer is that there is another factor that influences the relative stability of a system. It is called **entropy**. Entropy is a measure of the disorder or randomness of a system. The greater the degree of disorder, the greater the stability; and thus the total free energy of a system is the sum of the enthalpy and the entropy.

At this stage we can say no more, but if you proceed beyond this level with your studies of physics and chemistry, you will hear a lot more about it. It is a fascinating and essential idea in understanding the chemical changes in our environment.

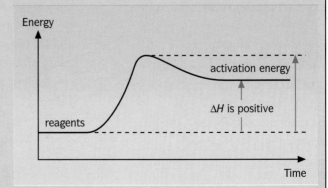

● **Figure 3.28** An energy pathway diagram for an endothermic reaction.

Catalysis

There is a third factor beside reagent concentration and temperature that influences reaction rate. It is catalysis. A **catalyst** is something added to a reaction that increases its rate, but does not itself change in concentration: the same amount remains after reaction as before. It is not true to say that the catalyst is unchanged. Sometimes it may not be changed. Sometimes its form may be quite different after the reaction to what it was before the reaction.

Catalysts increase reaction rates by lowering the activation barrier for the reaction without altering the products of the reaction. This is shown in *figure 3.30*. Catalysts enable a greater proportion of the molecules in a sample to be above the activation energy, as shown in the Boltzmann distribution in *figure 3.31*. How do catalysts bring this about? There are many ways in which catalysts can work, and we will now discuss these in some detail.

First, we need to distinguish between two forms of catalysis, homogeneous catalysis and heterogeneous catalysis. In **homogeneous catalysis**, the catalyst is present in the same phase as the reactants, often in aqueous solution. We have already seen a good example of homogeneous catalysis in the reaction of propanone with iodine. This reaction is acid-catalysed. The presence of hydrogen ions speeds up the reaction, but the acid concentration remains the same at the end of the reaction as at the

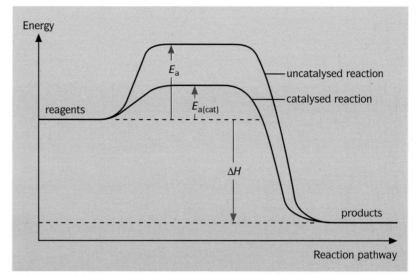

● *Figure 3.30* A catalyst lowers the activation energy, E_a.

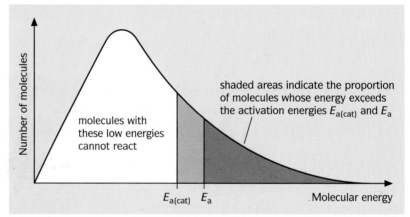

● *Figure 3.31* The lower activation energy does not alter the Boltzmann distribution; however, it does increase the number of molecules with energies above the activation energy.

beginning (as in *figure 3.18*, page 51):

$$CH_3COCH_3(aq) + I_2(aq) \xrightarrow{\text{H}^+(aq)} CH_3COCH_2I(aq) + HI(aq)$$

In **heterogeneous catalysis**, the catalyst is in a different phase to the reactants. The reaction occurs at an interface between the two phases, for example between molecules of a gas on the atoms at the surface of a solid. Many gas-phase reactions are catalysed by the presence of a finely divided solid, often containing metal ions. These are called **contact catalysts**. The accelerated reaction occurs on the metallic surface. A good example of this is the Haber process for the production of ammonia from nitrogen and hydrogen:

$$N_2(g) + 3H_2(g) \xrightarrow{\text{iron}} 2NH_3(g)$$

The catalyst is iron. (We will look at this reaction in more detail when we consider equilibria in chapter 4.)

Stage	Reaction	Plan view	Side view
Adsorption	$NH_3(g) \xrightarrow[\text{fast}]{W(s)} NH_3(W)$ (W is tungsten, $NH_3(W)$ means ammonia is adsorbed on the surface of tungsten). At this stage the rate is proportional to the concentration of ammonia rate $\propto [NH_3]$		
		We can imagine the molecules of ammonia landing on the surface of the tungsten, like little space invaders	
Reaction on the surface	$2NH_3(W) \xrightarrow[\text{fast}]{} N_2(W) + 3H_2(W)$ Now the rate is proportional to the square of the concentration of ammonia molecules (there are two molecules per reaction step) rate $\propto [NH_3]^2$		
		Attractive forces between the adsorbed molecules and the metal atoms help break the covalent bonds within the ammonia molecules. Other bonds form, resulting in the formation of nitrogen and hydrogen	
Desorption	$N_2(W) + 3H_2(W) \xrightarrow[\text{slow}]{} N_2(g) + 3H_2(g)$ The escape of the molecules that form on the surface is slow. It is the rate-determining step. This is the step that matters – see car parking analogy on the right. The rate is not proportional to the concentration of ammonia – it is zeroth-order with respect to ammonia. Unreacted ammonia molecules also escape but more take their place as soon as a gap is vacant		
		This is the slow step. Newly formed molecules of hydrogen and nitrogen escape from the surface of the tungsten. No fresh molecules of ammonia can be adsorbed until there is space available. It is rather like trying to park a car in a city car park. The parking rate is fast at first until all places are taken. From then on the parking rate depends upon the rate at which other cars leave	

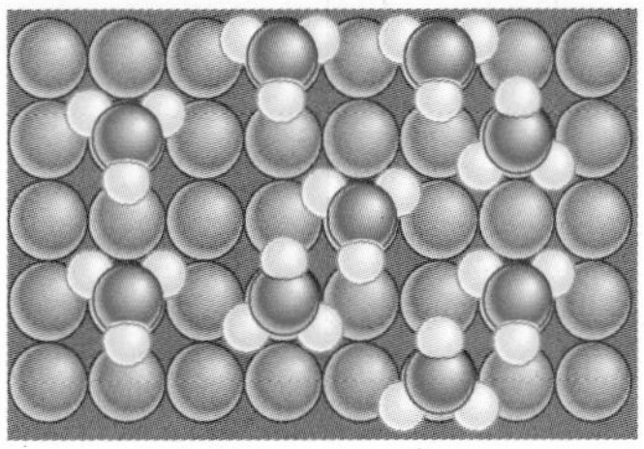

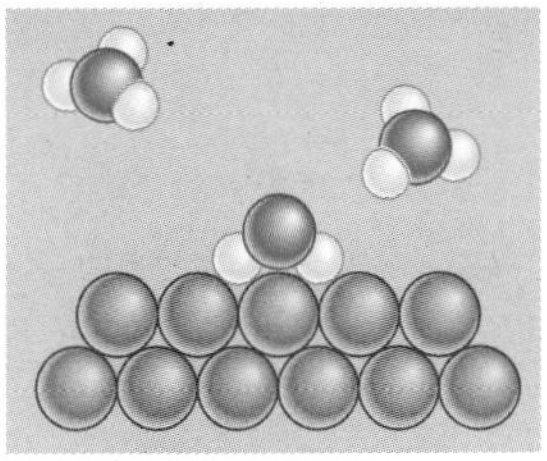

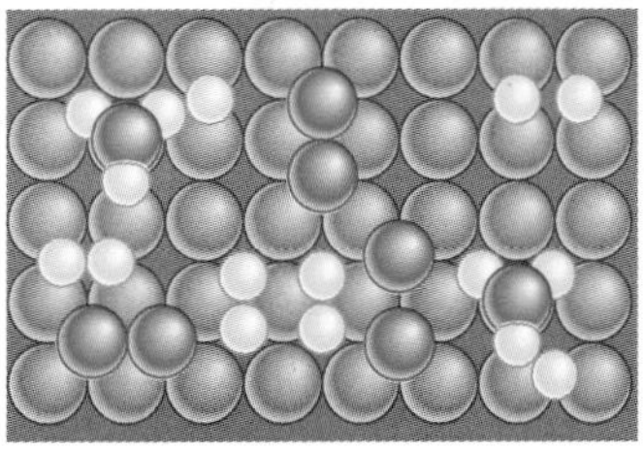

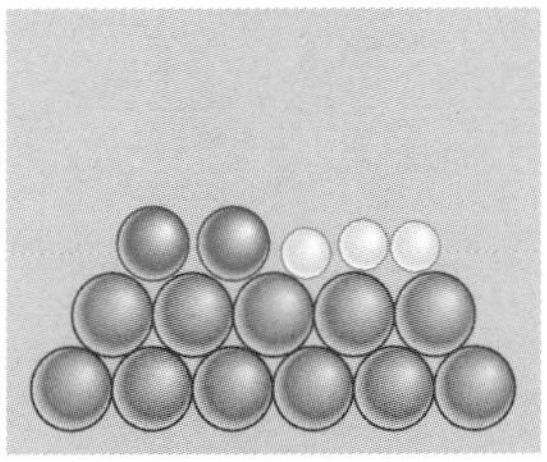

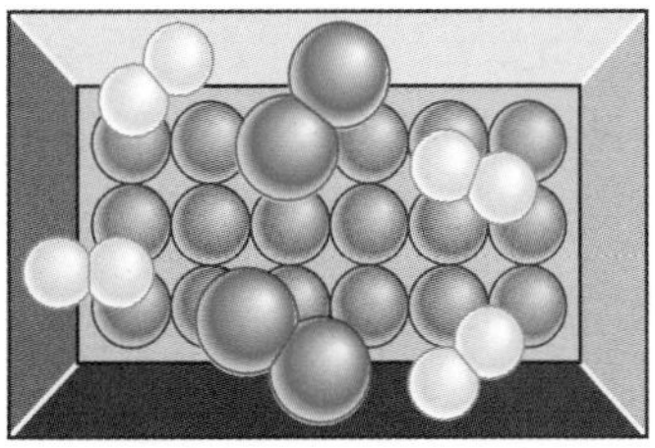

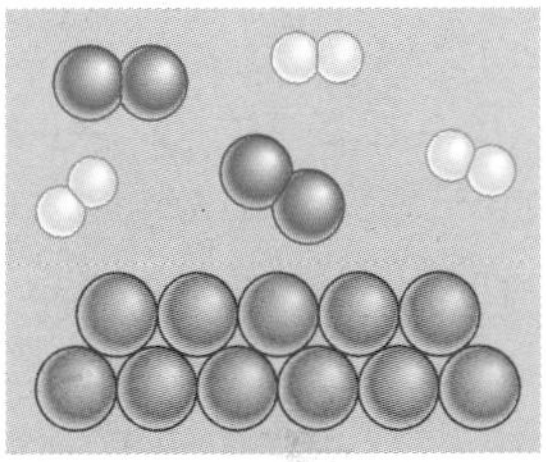

● **Figure 3.32** A model for the catalytic decomposition of ammonia gas on tungsten.

The nature of the surface of the catalyst is crucial. How it works is the subject of a great deal of research – better catalysts may mean more product in a given time, lower energy demands, and, increasingly these days, better environmental control. A model of one heterogeneous catalysis is shown in *figure 3.32*. (Further examples of industrial catalysis are included in the questions at the end of this chapter.)

Catalytic converters

Emission of toxic exhaust gases from cars may be controlled by catalytic converters. Exhaust gases produce the pollutants carbon monoxide, nitrogen dioxide and unburnt hydrocarbons (*table 3.9*).

The catalytic converter helps to promote the following reactions.

■ The oxidation of carbon monoxide to carbon dioxide:

$$2CO(g) + O_2(g) \longrightarrow 2CO_2(g)$$

■ The reduction of nitrogen monoxide back to nitrogen:

$$2NO(g) \rightleftharpoons N_2(g) + O_2(g)$$

■ The oxidation of hydrocarbons to water and carbon dioxide. For example:

$$2C_6H_6(g) + 15O_2(g)$$
$$\longrightarrow 12CO_2(g) + 6H_2O(l)$$

The catalyst can be expensive, as it is made of an alloy of platinum and rhodium. Research to reduce costs has led to oxides of transition metals like chromium being used instead. Catalysts may be poisoned – rendered useless – by lead. Organic lead compounds such as tetraethyl lead, $Pb(C_2H_5)_4$, were once added to petrol to increase engine efficiency. However, improved engine design now allows the use of lead-free petrol – a case of engineers and chemists working together to cure a problem caused by engineers and chemists curing another!

Enzymes: Nature's super-catalysts

A vast array of enormously significant catalysts are provided by enzymes. They occur in living systems and allow reactions to occur at relatively low temperatures like 310 K (your body temperature), and at relatively low pressures. They are organic compounds that catalyse the reactions involved in the vital processes within animals and plants. Enzyme deficiencies or disorders are closely connected with many diseases. Industrial processes are often improved by the addition of enzyme catalysts.

Enzymes are proteins, long chains of amino acids linked together by peptide bonds as shown in *figure 3.33*. They may contain several hundred amino acids linked in this way. Relative molecular masses are usually in the range of 50 000. These long chains are never flat, because hydrogen bonds are formed between amino acids in the chain. The most common way of folding the chain is the α-helix *(figure 3.34)*. Only parts of the chain may fold this way; other parts may fold in different ways. More than this, the chain may fold again into a complex shape. This three-dimensional shape is held firmly by the hydrogen bonds. This is very important for enzymes, because it brings into close proximity the group of amino acids that holds the substrate molecule in the correct position for it to be changed into the product.

Enzymes are chiral and thus can differentiate between the left- and right-handed molecules in a mixture. This is very useful in the pharmaceutical industry. The enzyme tyrosinase specifically converts L-tyrosine into L-DOPA, a right-handed molecule which is important in the treatment of Parkinson's disease *(figure 3.35)*. The use of a

Name of gas	Formula	Origin	Effect
Carbon monoxide	CO	Incomplete combustion of hydrocarbons in petrol, for example: $C_8H_{18}(g) + 12O_2(g)$ $\longrightarrow CO(g) + 7CO_2(g) + 9H_2O(l)$	Poisonous gas that combines with oxygen-carrying haemoglobin in the blood, and prevents oxygen from being carried
Nitrogen dioxide	NO_2	Atmospheric nitrogen and oxygen combine under the high-temperature conditions of the engine to form nitrogen monoxide: $N_2(g) + O_2(g) \rightleftharpoons 2NO(g)$ This is oxidised rapidly in the atmosphere to form nitrogen dioxide: $2NO(g) + O_2(g) \longrightarrow 2NO_2(g)$	Forms dilute nitric acid when it dissolves in water – in the air or in your lungs. Nitrogen dioxide is also involved in the formation of photochemical smog
Hydrocarbons	C_xH_y	Some hydrocarbons in petrol may not be combusted at all	Some hydrocarbons (for example benzene) are toxic and may cause cancer

● *Table 3.9* Pollutants in exhaust fumes

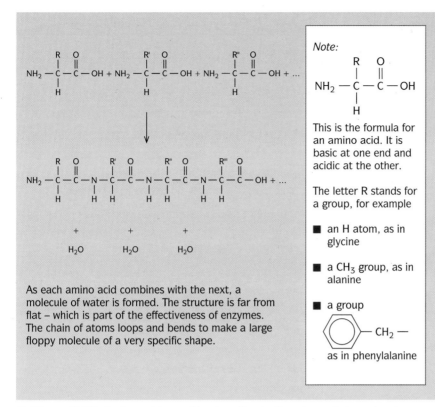

As each amino acid combines with the next, a molecule of water is formed. The structure is far from flat – which is part of the effectiveness of enzymes. The chain of atoms loops and bends to make a large floppy molecule of a very specific shape.

Note:

This is the formula for an amino acid. It is basic at one end and acidic at the other.

The letter R stands for a group, for example

- an H atom, as in glycine

- a CH$_3$ group, as in alanine

- a group $\bigcirc$–CH$_2$– as in phenylalanine

● **Figure 3.33** Amino acids combine together to form long-chain molecules of great variety.

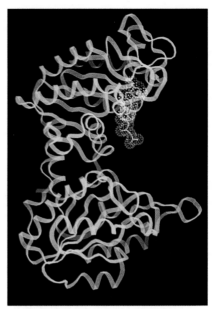

● **Figure 3.34** Three-dimensional representation of the enzyme phosphoglycerate kinase (yellow) bonded to a molecule of ATP (green). Kinase enzymes catalyse the transfer of phosphoryl groups from one substrate (usually ATP) to another. This enzyme contains several regions coiled as α-helices; one is clearly visible at the top.

mixture of the optical isomers (L-DOPA and D-DOPA) would lead to undesirable side-effects.

Enzymes are involved in almost every reaction in your body. For example, they help you to digest food and protect you from dangerous waste products that form in your body, such as hydrogen peroxide. This substance is produced as a result of oxidation reactions in cells, and is very toxic. It is broken down by catalase, the fastest acting enzyme known, to water and oxygen.

Enzymes are used in industrial processes to catalyse biochemical reactions. One very useful reaction concerns the conversion of

D-glucose into a mixture of D-glucose and D-fructose called 'high fructose syrup'. Fructose is sweeter than glucose, and a mixture of both is sweeter than either. Millions of tonnes of this syrup are produced for the food industry. The catalyst, glucose isomerase, occurs inside certain microbial cells. It is 'immobilised' within the cells by careful heat treatment, or extraction and adsorption onto an ion exchange resin. This keeps the enzyme on a solid structure so that it can be recovered by filtration and used time and time again.

L-tyrosine → (tyrosinase / oxygen) → L-DOPA   R-DOPA not produced

● **Figure 3.35** The chiral nature of the enzyme tyrosinase ensures that the L-isomer of DOPA (3,4-dihydroxyphenylalanine) is formed, not the R-isomer.

SUMMARY

- The rate of reaction is a measure of the rate of use of reactants and the rate of production of products. It is measured in units of concentration per unit time ($mol\,dm^{-3}\,s^{-1}$).

- The rate of reaction is related to the concentrations of the reactants by the rate equation, which (for two reactants A and B) is of the form:

  rate = $k[A]^x[B]^y$

  where k is the rate constant, [A] and [B] are the concentrations of the reactants, x is the order of reaction with respect to A and y is the order of reaction with respect to B.

- The rate equation cannot be predicted from the stoichiometric equation.

- The overall order of reaction is the sum of the individual orders of the reactants. For the example above:

  overall order = $x + y$

- The order of reaction with respect to a particular reactant indicates how many molecules of that reactant participate in the slow step (rate-determining step) of a reaction mechanism. This slow step determines the overall rate of reaction.

- The order of reaction may be determined by the initial-rates method, in which the initial rate is measured for several experiments using different concentrations of reactants. One concentration is changed whilst the others are fixed, so that a clear and systematic set of results is obtained.

- The order of reaction may also be determined from a single experiment, in which a concentration–time graph is recorded over a period of time. Tangents taken from several points on the graph give a measure of how the reaction rate changes with time. The reaction rate at a particular point is the gradient of the graph at that point.

- The half-life of a first-order reaction is the time taken for the initial concentration of a reactant to halve, and it is independent of the concentration(s) of reactant(s).

- The activation energy of a reaction is the minimum initial input of energy required to start the process of bond breaking.

- The Boltzmann distribution represents the numbers of molecules in a sample with particular energies.

- The rate of a reaction increases with increasing temperature, because more molecules have energies close to, or over, the activation energy.

- A catalyst lowers the activation energy of a reaction, so more molecules have energies close to, or over, the activation energy. Hence a catalyst increases the rate of a reaction.

- Catalysts are either *homogeneous*, in which case they are in the same phase as the reactants, or *heterogeneous*, in which case they are in a different phase to the reactants.

- Enzymes may behave as biological catalysts.

- Catalysts are important economically because they increase rates of production of important industrial chemicals.

- Catalytic converters are fitted to cars to reduce emissions of harmful exhaust gases. They contain a platinum/rhodium catalyst that promotes the conversion of harmful gases into less harmful products.

Question

1 A good example of the effect of catalysts is the decomposition of hydrogen peroxide to oxygen:

$$2H_2O_2(aq) \longrightarrow 2H_2O(l) + O_2(g)$$

This occurs slowly at room temperatures. The reaction is accelerated by the addition of a small amount of water-soluble iodide. The reaction mechanism is as follows:

$$H_2O_2(aq) + I^-(aq) \longrightarrow IO^-(aq) + H_2O(l)$$
(slow)

$$H_2O_2(aq) + IO^-(aq) \longrightarrow H_2O(l) + O_2(g) + I^-(aq)$$
(fast)

Deduce the rate equation from this reaction mechanism.

Chapter four

Chemical equilibria

By the end of this chapter you should be able to:

1 understand what is meant by the terms *reversible reaction* and *dynamic equilibrium*;

2 use Le Chatelier's principle to explain the effects on an equilibrium of changes in temperature, concentration or pressure;

3 understand how changes in temperature, concentration or pressure, or the presence of a catalyst, may affect the equilibrium constant for a reaction;

4 produce expressions for equilibrium constants, K_c and K_p, in terms of concentrations and pressures respectively;

5 calculate the values of equilibrium constants in terms of concentrations or partial pressures;

6 calculate the quantities of reactants and products present at equilibrium;

7 describe and explain the conditions used in both the Haber process and the Contact process.

Equilibrium – a state of balanced change

The notion of a system being in equilibrium is a familiar one. You can stir salt into water until no more will dissolve. At this point the saturated solution is in equilibrium with the undissolved solid. However, although the concentration of the saturated solution stays the same, the ions and molecules are in a constant state of motion. The equilibrium is dynamic. Ions in the crystal lattice of the undissolved solid continue to go into solution. However, they are immediately replaced elsewhere in the lattice by the same numbers and kinds of ion. The situation is one of continued but balanced change *(figure 4.1)*.

A similar situation exists when you close a cylinder of propane gas, in a camping gas stove for example.

Evaporation and condensation go on until the two phases are in equilibrium with one another. Again the equilibrium is dynamic. At equilibrium some of the molecules of liquid propane are evaporating, but only at the same rate as molecules of gaseous propane are condensing *(figure 4.1)*.

In both cases it is possible to disturb the balance of the system. In the first case, for example, you could shift the equilibrium by changing the temperature or by introducing further amounts of solvent. Whatever is done, the system readjusts to regain an equilibrium.

Equilibrium and chemical change

If you heat calcium carbonate it decomposes, forming calcium oxide and carbon dioxide:

$$CaCO_3(s) \longrightarrow CaO(s) + CO_2(g)$$

On the other hand, if you leave calcium oxide in an atmosphere of carbon dioxide, the reverse reaction occurs, and calcium carbonate forms:

$$CaO(s) + CO_2(g) \longrightarrow CaCO_3(s)$$

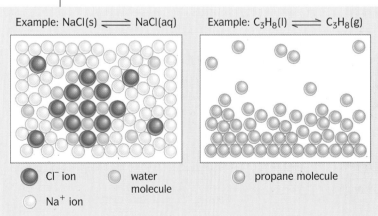

Example: $NaCl(s) \rightleftharpoons NaCl(aq)$ Example: $C_3H_8(l) \rightleftharpoons C_3H_8(g)$

○ Cl^- ion   ○ water molecule   ○ propane molecule
○ Na^+ ion

● **Figure 4.1** Two physical equilibria. In both situations there is a constant interchange of particles, which maintains a steady balance. In one case, ions leave a crystal structure, while others join it. In the other case, molecules escape from the crush in a liquid to relative isolation in a gas, while others leave the gas to join the liquid.

If these substances are put in a sealed container at a high temperature (say 700 K) and left to get on with it, an equilibrium is set up. Both of the above reactions occur until a balance is reached. At this point the rate of formation of calcium carbonate equals its rate of decomposition.

All chemical reactions can reach equilibrium, a situation where the reactants are in equilibrium with the products. Again, these are dynamic equilibria: reagents are constantly being converted to products, and vice versa. At equilibrium the rate of the forward process is the same as that of the backward one. The idea that *all* chemical reactions can reach equilibrium seems to conflict with experience, e.g. the burning of magnesium in air. In many cases the degree of conversion of reactants to products is so large that, at the conclusion of the reaction, no reactants can be detected by normal analytical means. At other times two reagents, e.g. the nitrogen and oxygen in the air, do not seem to react at all. Such reactions are often considered to be irreversible one-way reactions under those conditions.

Suppose for example we mix equimolecular amounts of hydrogen with either chlorine or bromine. The green colour of the chlorine or the orange colour of the bromine disappears, and we are left with hydrogen chloride or hydrogen bromide. Both reactions go to apparent completion as indicated by these equations:

$$H_2(g) + Cl_2(g) \longrightarrow 2HCl(g)$$
$$H_2(g) + Br_2(g) \longrightarrow 2HBr(g)$$

When we mix hydrogen gas and iodine vapour, however, we find that the violet colour of the iodine persists. There is an equilibrium set up between the three components in which all three are present in significant amounts, as shown in the equation below and in *figure 4.2*:

$$H_2(g) + I_2(g) \rightleftharpoons 2HI(g)$$

The equation tells us that when a molecule of hydrogen reacts with a molecule of iodine, two molecules of hydrogen iodide are formed.

It also enables us to examine the reaction in reverse. If two molecules of hydrogen iodide dissociate (i.e. split apart), then a molecule each of hydrogen and iodine are formed.

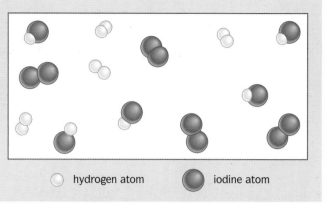

hydrogen atom   iodine atom

● **Figure 4.2** A snapshot of the dynamic equilibrium between hydrogen gas, iodine gas and hydrogen iodide gas.

Finding the balance

Iodine gas is purple. The more there is, the deeper the shade of purple. A spectrophotometer can be used to measure this intensity, and hence the concentration of iodine in a reaction vessel.

The equilibrium can be approached from either side:

■ by using a mixture of hydrogen gas and iodine gas (purple), which reacts to form colourless hydrogen iodide, *or*
■ by using pure hydrogen iodide, which dissociates to form hydrogen and iodine.

Figure 4.3 illustrates what happens when 5.00 moles of each of hydrogen molecules and iodine molecules react at 500 K. As time passes, the purple colour of the iodine fades until a steady state is reached. Analysis shows that the final amount of the iodine is 0.68 moles. There must also be 0.68 moles of hydrogen left, as the equation shows. The remaining 4.32 moles of each gas have been converted to 8.64 moles of hydrogen iodide molecules.

SAQ 4.1

The same equilibrium can be achieved starting with 10 moles of hydrogen iodide molecules *(figure 4.4)*. Describe what happens and satisfy yourself that, if 0.68 moles of iodine molecules are found to be in the final mixture, then there must be 8.64 moles of hydrogen iodide molecules present.

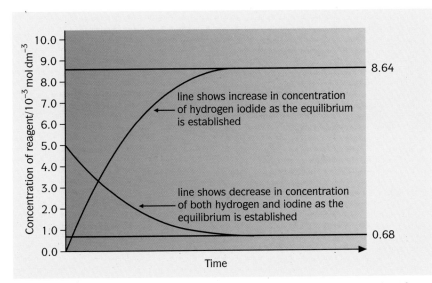

● **Figure 4.3** The changes in the concentrations of reagents as five moles of each of hydrogen and iodine react to form an equilibrium with hydrogen iodide in a vessel of volume 1 m³.

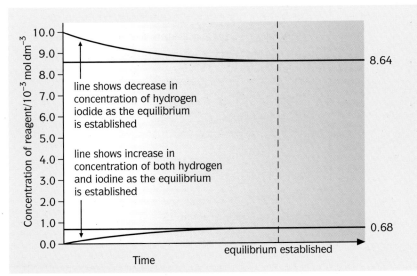

● **Figure 4.4** The changes in the concentrations of reagents as ten moles of hydrogen iodide react to form an equilibrium with hydrogen and iodine gases.

$[H_2]/mol\,dm^{-3}$	$[I_2]/mol\,dm^{-3}$	$[HI]/mol\,dm^{-3}$	$\dfrac{[HI]^2}{[H_2][I_2]}$
0.68×10^{-3}	0.68×10^{-3}	8.64×10^{-3}	161
0.50×10^{-3}	0.50×10^{-3}	6.30×10^{-3}	159
1.10×10^{-3}	1.10×10^{-3}	13.9×10^{-3}	160
1.10×10^{-3}	2.00×10^{-3}	18.8×10^{-3}	161
2.50×10^{-3}	0.65×10^{-3}	16.1×10^{-3}	160

● **Table 4.1** Equilibrium concentrations of hydrogen, $H_2(g)$, iodine, $I_2(g)$, and hydrogen iodide, $HI(g)$, at 500 K

We can find the concentrations of the three components in any equilibrium by spectroscopically analysing the amount of iodine present in the equilibrium mixture, knowing the amount of hydrogen and iodine we had to start with. *Table 4.1* shows some values obtained. The fourth column shows the value of $[HI]^2/[H_2][I_2]$, which, as you can see, is constant (allowing for experimental error). It is called the **equilibrium constant**, K_c, for the reaction, and in this case it is given by the square of the equilibrium concentration of the hydrogen iodide, divided by the product of the equilibrium concentrations of the hydrogen and the iodine.

In general, if w, x, y and z are numbers of moles, and A, B, C and D are the reactants and products, and if the equation is:

$$wA + xB \rightleftharpoons yC + zD$$

then

$$K_c = \frac{[C]^y[D]^z}{[A]^w[B]^x}$$

Notice that if the concentrations of C and D are high compared to A and B, then K_c is also high. High values of K_c indicate a high percentage of products compared to reactants.

Clearly the units of K_c are going to be tricky, and will vary from case to case. For K_c in *table 4.1*, we are dividing a concentration squared by the product of two concentrations, so in this case it has no units – it is just a number.

SAQ 4.2

What do low values for K_c tell you about a chemical equilibrium?

We shall now do an example. Consider the reaction of nitrogen and hydrogen to produce ammonia (the Haber process):

$$N_2(g) + 3H_2(g) \rightleftharpoons 2NH_3(g)$$

For this reaction, at equilibrium:

$$K_c = \frac{[NH_3(g)]^2}{[N_2(g)]\,[H_2(g)]^3}$$

The units for K_c are given by:

$$\text{units } (K_c) = \frac{(\text{mol dm}^{-3})^2}{(\text{mol dm}^{-3})\,(\text{mol dm}^{-3})^3}$$

$$= \frac{\text{mol}^2\,\text{dm}^{-6}}{\text{mol dm}^{-3}\,\text{mol}^3\,\text{dm}^{-9}}$$

$$= \text{mol}^{-2}\,\text{dm}^6$$

SAQ 4.3

Write the formula for K_c for each of the following reactions, and work out the units for K_c assuming the concentrations of the gases are measured in mol dm^{-3}.

a $2NO_2(g) \rightleftharpoons N_2O_4(g)$

b $2NO(g) + O_2(g) \rightleftharpoons 2NO_2(g)$

c $4NH_3(g) + 5O_2(g) \rightleftharpoons 4NO(g) + 6H_2O(g)$

Le Chatelier's principle

The adjustment of concentration to maintain K_c constant at a given temperature is a manifestation of an important principle first put forward by the French chemist Le Chatelier in 1884 and known (strangely enough!) as **Le Chatelier's principle**: when any of the conditions affecting the position of a dynamic equilibrium are changed, then the position of that equilibrium will shift so as to minimise the change.

Le Chatelier's principle applies to dynamic chemical equilibria. It is as if each equilibrium understands when it is being changed, and adjusts to keep the change to a minimum. In the hydrogen plus iodine reaction above, temperature is constant, and concentration can change. Any change in concentration of any of the substances taking part in the equilibrium causes the position of the equilibrium to shift so that it minimises that

change in concentration. For example, if we add extra hydrogen iodide to the system at equilibrium, the equilibrium shifts so that hydrogen iodide is used up, more hydrogen and iodine are produced, and K_c is kept the same. You can check this out by comparing lines 3 and 4 in *table 4.1*. You could also look at the mathematics of the situation – see *box 4A*.

Box 4A Le Chatelier's principle: the mathematics of compensation

We know from experimental results that the reaction

$$H_2(g) + I_2(g) \rightleftharpoons 2HI(g)$$

has an equilibrium constant

$$K_c = \frac{[HI(g)]^2}{[H_2(g)][I_2(g)]}$$

If [HI] increases, K_c increases. To compensate, $[H_2][I_2]$ must also increase. This requires a shift to the left in the reaction as written, i.e. a greater concentration of hydrogen and iodine in the equilibrium.

In another situation, suppose that the concentration of hydrogen in the equilibrium was reduced. Without compensation, K_c would get bigger. To stop this happening, $[HI]^2$ would have to reduce, i.e. [HI] would have to decrease. The equilibrium as written would shift to the left.

SAQ 4.4

Work out how increasing the concentration of iodine would affect the equilibrium in the reaction of hydrogen with iodine.

The effect of temperature on equilibria

K_c varies with temperature, so it is always important to specify at what temperature K_c has been defined. *Table 4.2* shows the way K_c varies with temperature for the three reactions between hydrogen and the halogens chlorine, bromine and iodine.

Le Chatelier's principle can be used to interpret the effect of temperature on the equilibrium constant of a reaction. Consider the equilibrium for an exothermic reaction (like the reactions in

Reaction	Temperature/K	K_c
$H_2(g) + Cl_2(g) \rightleftharpoons 2HCl(g)$	300	4.0×10^{31}
	500	4.0×10^{18}
	1000	3.1×10^8
$H_2(g) + Br_2(g) \rightleftharpoons 2HBr(g)$	300	1.0×10^{17}
	500	1.3×10^{10}
	1000	3.8×10^4
$H_2(g) + I_2(g) \rightleftharpoons 2HI(g)$	300	794
	500	160
	1000	54

● **Table 4.2** Equilibrium constants and their variation with temperature for the hydrogen–halogen reactions

table 4.2), summarised as follows:

reactants $\rightleftharpoons$ products;

ΔH is negative

Suppose the temperature of the reaction is lowered. There is a consequent reduction in heat energy in the system of reactants and products. According to Le Chatelier's principle, the equilibrium should shift in order to compensate for this reduction. This can only happen if more heat energy is generated, i.e. if more product is formed. Hence K_c will increase and the equilibrium position will move to the right.

SAQ 4.5

Produce similar arguments to predict what should happen to K_c and the equilibrium position if:

a the temperature of an exothermic equilibrium was increased;

b the temperature of an endothermic equilibrium was increased;

c the temperature of an endothermic equilibrium was decreased.

To summarise, we can write our findings like this:

■ For *exothermic reactions*: *increase* in temperature leads to less product formation, and K_c decreases
decrease in temperature leads to more product formation, and K_c increases

Example $2SO_2(g) + O_2(g) \rightleftharpoons 2SO_3(g)$

■ For *endothermic reactions*: *increase* in temperature leads to more product formation, and K_c increases
decrease in temperature leads to less product formation, and K_c decreases

Example $CaCO_3(s) \rightleftharpoons CaO(s) + CO_2(g)$

The effect of pressure on equilibria

Pressure has virtually no effect on the chemistry of solids and liquids. As shown in *figure 4.5*, pressure does not affect the concentration of solids and liquids – the molecules concerned are already in contact and it is difficult to push them closer together.

Pressure does have significant effects on the chemistry of reacting gases. As *figure 4.6* shows, the concentrations of gases increase with an increase in pressure, and decrease with a decrease in pressure. Since chemical equilibria are influenced by concentration changes, pressure changes also have an effect on equilibria where one or more of the reagents is a gas. However, a change in pressure *does not* affect the equilibrium constant.

Again we can apply Le Chatelier's principle to predict how pressure change will affect an equilibrium. Imagine a reaction in the gaseous phase where two molecules, A and B, combine to form a single molecule, C:

$A(g) + B(g) \rightleftharpoons C(g)$

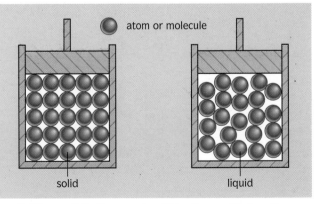

● **Figure 4.5** Pressure has little, if any, effect on the concentrations of solids and liquids.

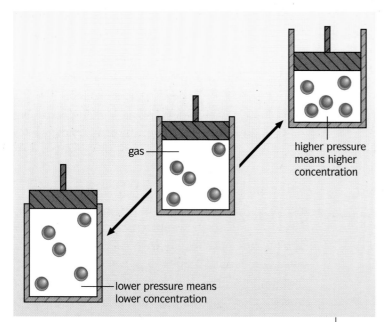

● **Figure 4.6** Pressure has a considerable effect on the concentrations of gases.

The situation is illustrated in *figure 4.7.*

It helps to remember that the pressure of a gas depends on the number of molecules in a given volume of the gas. The greater the number of molecules, the greater the number of collisions per second, and hence the greater the pressure of the gas. In the reaction above, when the pressure is increased *the equilibrium shifts so as to minimise this increase*, that is, to reduce the pressure overall.

Therefore, there must be fewer molecules present than before. This can only happen if A and B molecules react to make more molecules of C.

This reasoning is summarised below. This is shown as a list to summarise the effects of increasing and decreasing the pressure on reactions in which **a** there are fewer molecules on the right of the equilibrium, and **b** there are more molecules on the right of the equilibrium.

■ For *fewer molecules on the right*   *increase* in pressure leads to more product formation *decrease* in pressure leads to less product formation

    Example $2SO_2(g) + O_2(g) \rightleftharpoons 2SO_3(g)$

■ For *more molecules on the right*   *increase* in pressure leads to less product formation *decrease* in pressure leads to more product formation

    Example $N_2O_4(g) \rightleftharpoons 2NO_2(g)$

The effect of catalysts on equilibria

As you know, a catalyst reduces the activation energy of a reaction, and hence speeds it up. A catalyst affects the rate of reaction, but does not itself get involved in the stoichiometry of the reaction. More catalyst could mean a faster reaction, one in which an equilibrium was established more quickly, *but with no more product and no less product being formed.* Therefore, the catalyst does not figure in the equilibrium constant K_c, so the presence of a catalyst has no effect on the position of an equilibrium.

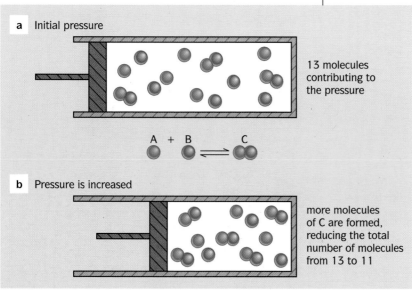

● **Figure 4.7** An increase in pressure in this case causes the equilibrium to shift to the right, to produce more molecules of C than before, but fewer molecules in the reaction vessel.

An equilibrium of importance: the Haber process

We will now gather together these ideas using a reaction that is important from the theoretical, the practical and the industrial points of view. It is the Haber process for the 'fixation' of atmospheric nitrogen. We need large amounts of nitrogen compounds, particularly for fertilisers. Atmospheric nitrogen is the most plentiful and readily available source. At the same time, it cannot be used directly in the gaseous form; it needs to be 'fixed' into a chemically combined form to make a useful compound. The most obvious conversion would seem to be to ammonia. Unlike nitrogen, ammonia is a reactive gas readily soluble in water, is readily convertible to ammonium salts, and can be converted to nitric acid by the Ostwald process of oxidation.

The equation for the reaction to form ammonia is as follows:

$$N_2(g) + 3H_2(g) \rightleftharpoons 2NH_3(g);$$
$$\Delta H = -93 \, kJ \, mol^{-1}$$

The unreactive nature of nitrogen is, of course, a problem. Although the reaction is exothermic, the triple bond within nitrogen molecules lends them great strength, so the reaction has a high activation energy. How may the equilibrium be influenced to give good yields of ammonia? This problem was solved at the turn of this century by the German chemist Fritz Haber, and the process that he developed is essentially that still in use today.

The equilibrium constant for this reaction is

$$K_c = \frac{[NH_3]^2}{[N_2][H_2]^3}$$

At 273 K and 1 atmosphere pressure the equilibrium constant K_c is $2.7 \times 10^8 \, mol^{-2} dm^6$ (note the units, and make sure that you can derive them). The equilibrium position is well over to the right, and the conversion of nitrogen and hydrogen to ammonia is almost complete. The problem is that the reaction has a very high activation energy. The reaction is so extremely *slow* that it cannot even be observed.

The obvious thing to do would seem to be to increase the temperature, but by using Le Chatelier's principle we may reason that this will have an effect that will work against us. Since the reaction is exothermic, increase of temperature will drive the equilibrium to the left, and this effect is quite dramatic; at 373 K the percentage of ammonia resulting from an initial mixture of 1 volume of nitrogen and 3 volumes of hydrogen is 80%: at 673 K this percentage drops to 0.5%.

Pressure is another variable, and for the discussion so far we have assumed it to be kept at 1 atmosphere. We can reason, however, that increase of pressure will drive the equilibrium to the right. From Avogadro's hypothesis, we know that equal volumes of all gases under the same conditions of temperature and pressure contain the same number of molecules. One mole of any gas therefore occupies the same volume, $22.4 \, dm^{-3}$, at STP (STP stands for standard temperature, 298 K, and pressure, 1 atm = 101 kPa). From this we can deduce the proportions by volume of the gases in the equation below:

$$N_2(g) + 3H_2(g) \rightleftharpoons 2NH_3(g);$$

1 volume   3 volumes   2 volumes $\Delta H = -93 \, kJ \, mol^{-1}$

According to Le Chatelier's principle, an increase in pressure should drive the equilibrium to the right, since this will result in a decrease in volume. This is found in practice, and *table 4.3* gives the relevant figures. The answer therefore seems to be to run the reaction at as low a temperature and as high a pressure as possible. However, at low temperatures the rate of reaction is very slow, hence a compromise must be made between rate and temperature.

	Percentage of ammonia at equilibrium			
Temperature/K	25 atm	50 atm	100 atm	200 atm
373	91.7	94.5	96.7	98.4
573	27.4	39.6	53.1	66.7
773	2.9	5.6	10.5	18.3
973	0.9	1.2	3.4	8.7

● **Table 4.3** Percentage of ammonia in the equilibrium mixture at various temperatures and pressures

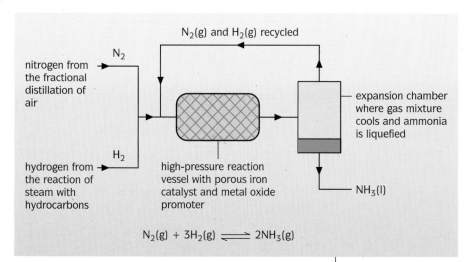

N2(g) and H2(g) recycled

nitrogen from the fractional distillation of air → N2

hydrogen from the reaction of steam with hydrocarbons → H2

high-pressure reaction vessel with porous iron catalyst and metal oxide promoter

expansion chamber where gas mixture cools and ammonia is liquefied

NH3(l)

$$N_2(g) + 3H_2(g) \rightleftharpoons 2NH_3(g)$$

● *Figure 4.8* The production of ammonia by the Haber process.

A further ploy to increase effectiveness is to use a catalyst that enables the reaction to reach equilibrium as quickly as possible. Porous iron, activated by the addition of other metal oxides and silicon oxide, is very effective.

The complexity of the Haber process problem, with its many variables affecting outcome in different ways, required extensive experimentation, as you can imagine, and led eventually to the conditions presently used for the reaction – a temperature in the range 673–813 K and a pressure in the range 80–350 atm. The unreacted hydrogen and nitrogen from the equilibrium are recirculated through the catalyst after the ammonia has been condensed out (*figure 4.8*). In this way, 1.5×10^{10} kg of ammonia are produced per year in the USA alone, of which 80% is used as fertiliser, either by direct application or through conversion to ammonium salts such as ammonium nitrate or ammonium sulphate.

As with all industrial processes, the economic factor in the Haber process must also be considered very carefully. It may well turn out, as it does in this case, that the optimum conditions may be very expensive to achieve. For example, building safe high-pressure reaction vessels is an expensive business. This itself requires research and development, all of which costs money. A compromise must be sought between maximum yield and lowest cost. This can vary on a regional basis, e.g. on the availability of cheap electricity, and the proximity to 'chemical plant' supplies and maintenance.

The Contact process

This is the process for making sulphuric acid, one of the chemical industry's most useful materials. Over 130 000 000 tonnes of it are produced worldwide every year. Sulphuric acid is both the acid used in car batteries and the cheapest of your lab bench acids, but its main use is for making fertilisers (*figure 4.9*).

The aims of any company manufacturing sulphuric acid are to make as much profit as possible and to minimise pollution. Companies which pollute the environment can be fined or closed down, so chemical engineers must design systems to keep well within permitted levels. They must also save energy at every stage. We shall now discuss the three stages of the Contact process.

The manufacture of sulphur dioxide

Sulphur is melted, and sprayed into air heated to around 1000°C. The sulphur burns violently,

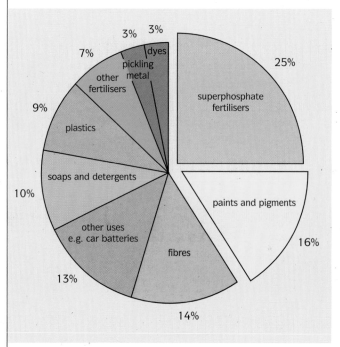

● *Figure 4.9* The uses of sulphuric acid.

forming sulphur dioxide:

$$S(g) + O_2(g) \longrightarrow SO_2(g);$$
$$\Delta H^{\ominus}_{298} = -297 \, \text{kJ} \, \text{mol}^{-1}$$

The heat produced is not wasted. It is used to help run the rest of the factory. Note that the enthalpy change quoted is for 298 K, and will not be the same under the typical reaction conditions.

SAQ 4.6

The burning of sulphur produces a mixture of gases, about 10% sulphur dioxide and 10% oxygen by volume. What does the remaining 80% of this gas mixture consist of, and what do these figures tell you about the combustion of the sulphur?

The manufacture of sulphur trioxide

The mixture of sulphur dioxide and oxygen is converted into sulphur trioxide, making use of this reaction:

$$SO_2(g) + O_2(g) \rightleftharpoons SO_3(g);$$
$$\Delta H^{\ominus}_{298} = -98 \, \text{kJ} \, \text{mol}^{-1}$$

Note the key features of this equilibrium:

- there is an overall decrease of volume;
- the reaction is exothermic.

SAQ 4.7

Use Le Chatelier's principle to answer the following questions, with a view to maximising the percentage of sulphur trioxide produced in the equilibrium.

a Should the sulphur trioxide be removed as it is formed?

b Should the temperature be high or low?

c Should the pressure be high or low?

Catalysts have been developed to increase the rate of reaction. Platinum has been used, but this is very expensive and easily poisoned (rendered ineffective) by impurities such as arsenic. Vanadium(V) oxide, V_2O_5, is preferred. It is made more effective by traces of

potassium sulphate, K_2SO_4 – a 'promoter', not a catalyst itself.

Figure 4.10 summarises the conditions at this stage. Note how the conditions produce a compromise between a number of needs:

- the need to shift the equilibrium in favour of sulphur trioxide;
- the need to increase the rate of reaction;
- the need to keep the costs of energy and plant low.

The manufacture of sulphuric acid

Sulphur trioxide reacts with water to form sulphuric acid:

$$H_2O(l) + SO_3(g) \longrightarrow H_2SO_4(aq);$$
$$\Delta H = -130 \, \text{kJ} \, \text{mol}^{-1}$$

With water alone the reaction produces a fine corrosive mist of sulphuric acid. It cannot be condensed and can be a dangerous pollutant. Instead the sulphur trioxide is absorbed in 98% sulphuric acid forming **oleum**, a dense oily liquid that is a solution of sulphur trioxide in sulphuric acid. The oleum is diluted with water to obtain the required concentration of sulphuric acid – a highly exothermic reaction, which requires careful control.

Some uses of sulphuric acid

Sulphuric acid is used to make hydrogen fluoride, a highly reactive acid used for polishing in the glass industry, preparing the surface of stainless steel

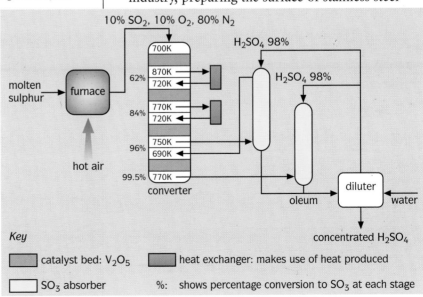

● **Figure 4.10** The Contact process.

products, and manufacturing anti-inflammatory drugs.

$$CaF_2(s) + H_2SO_4(aq) \longrightarrow CaSO_4(s) + 2HF(g)$$
fluorspar

The gas is liquefied by cooling it, and purified by fractional distillation.

Sulphuric acid is also involved in the manufacture of phosphoric acid, which is itself used to make phosphate fertilisers.

$$Ca_3(PO_4)_2 + 3H_2SO_4(aq)$$
$$\longrightarrow 2H_3PO_4(aq) + 3CaSO_4(s)$$

Phosphoric acid is an ingredient of drain cleaners and popular cola drinks. You have been warned!

Often, sulphuric acid is a component in a series of reactions to make useful products, for example dyes and detergents.

K_c or not K_c?

So far we have expressed equilibrium constants in terms of concentrations, and hence we use K_c. But for gaseous equilibria, an alternative expression, K_p, can be used. This makes use of pressures instead of concentrations, which in the gaseous state means much the same thing.

Imagine a box containing a gas, X, at pressure $p(X)$, and an identical box containing a gas, Y, at pressure $p(Y)$. If we assume that X does not react with Y, we can add all of gas Y to the box containing X, and they will mix. The pressure of the combined gases will (obviously) be larger than that of X or Y on its own. In fact, the total pressure, p, is given by:

$$p = p(X) + p(Y)$$

The pressures $p(X)$ and $p(Y)$ are referred to as the **partial pressures** of X and Y respectively. These partial pressures must be related in some way to the quantity of each gas present. Using the same example, if there are x moles of gas X and y moles of gas Y, then the partial pressures are related to the total pressure like this:

$$p(X) = \frac{x}{x + y} p$$

$$p(Y) = \frac{y}{x + y} p$$

Where $\frac{x}{x + y}$ and $\frac{y}{x + y}$ are called the **mole fractions** of X and Y respectively. Let's apply the idea of partial pressures to the Haber process (*figure 4.11*). The equation for the equilibrium is:

$$N_2(g) + 3H_2(g) = 2NH_3(g)$$

In the container in which the reaction takes place, the total pressure is given by:

$$p = p(N_2) + p(H_2) + p(NH_3)$$

In this situation, where all the chemicals present are gases, it is often easier to work with an equilibrium constant based on the partial pressures of the gases (called K_p, since we are working with pressures). The expression for K_p is formed in a very similar way to that of K_c for concentrations. At equilibrium:

$$K_p = \frac{\{p(NH_3)\}^2}{\{p(N_2)\}\{p(H_2)\}^3} \, Pa^{-2}$$

(The units are Pa^{-2} because we have Pa^2 on the top of the fraction and Pa^4 on the bottom.)

More generally, for the reaction

$$wA(g) + xB(g) \rightleftharpoons yC(g) + zD(g)$$

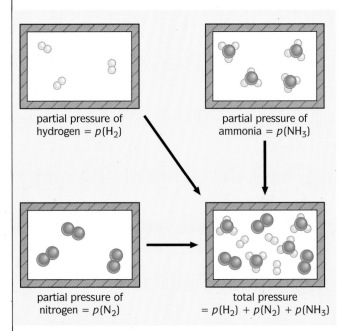

partial pressure of hydrogen = $p(H_2)$

partial pressure of ammonia = $p(NH_3)$

partial pressure of nitrogen = $p(N_2)$

total pressure = $p(H_2) + p(N_2) + p(NH_3)$

● **Figure 4.11** Each gas (hydrogen, nitrogen and ammonia) contributes its partial pressure to the total pressure.

the equilibrium constant is given by:

$$K_p = \frac{\{p(C)\}^y\{p(D)\}^z}{\{p(A)\}^w\{p(B)\}^x} \, Pa^{(y+z-w-x)}$$

SAQ 4.8

Write down the expression and units for K_p in the following equilibria:

a $N_2(g) + O_2(g) \rightleftharpoons 2NO(g)$

b $C_2H_4(g) + H_2O(g) \rightleftharpoons C_2H_5OH(g)$

Using K_c and K_p

You should try to develop a 'feel' for values of K_c and K_p, so that when you look at an equilibrium and the values for the equilibrium constants you can begin to imagine the extent of the formation of product from reactant. To some extent you have done this already, when looking at the trends in *tables 4.1* and *4.2*.

Another way is to tackle problems involving equilibrium constants – something expected of you in A-level examinations. Some examples are given below:

Question

Write the equation for the equilibrium established in the reaction between nitrogen and oxygen to produce nitrogen monoxide, NO. Write the formula for the equilibrium constant K_p for this reaction. What are the units for K_p?

Answer

Equation is

$$N_2(g) + O_2(g) \rightleftharpoons 2NO(g)$$

$$K_p = \frac{[NO]^2}{[N_2][O_2]} \qquad \frac{(Pa)^2}{Pa \times Pa}$$

The units all cancel, i.e. K_p is a number – it has no units.

Question

The value of the equilibrium constant for the above reaction at 293 K and 1 atmosphere pressure is 4.0×10^{-31}. What does this value tell you about the equilibrium?

Answer

The extremely low value indicates that at 293 K and one atmosphere the equilibrium is very much to the left-hand side, i.e. the reaction hardly occurs at all. (This is just as well – we live in a nitrogen/oxygen atmosphere, which would fuel this reaction!)

Box 4B Pollution and the equilibrium $N_2(g) + O_2(g) \rightleftharpoons 2NO(g)$

At 1100 K the value of K_c increases to 4×10^{-8}, still very small. However, calculations show that in $1\,cm^3$ of air at this temperature there would be around 2×10^{15} molecules of nitrogen oxide in an equilibrium – a small fraction of the total but enough to pose a pollution threat. Vehicle engines are a significant source of nitrogen oxide molecules. They contribute to a complex series of reactions with other molecules such as carbon monoxide, sulphur dioxide and hydrocarbons. Light energy plays its part, and the result can be a 'photochemical smog' of the form experienced in cities *(figure 4.12)*. The irritating chemicals produced include low-level ozone, O_3, and peroxyacetyl nitrates (PAN: $RCO \cdot O_2 \cdot NO_2$), which make your eyes water. Both of these are implicated in triggering asthma attacks.

Some photochemical smog occurs naturally. The haze of the Smoky Mountains in the USA seems to be caused by the reactions between oils from the pine forests and citrus groves with naturally occurring ozone. Atmospheric chemistry is both fascinating and complex: there will always be a need for research in this area. You can learn more about this subject in the *Environmental Chemistry* modular text.

● *Figure 4.12* Photochemical smog caused by light reacting with pollutant molecules.

Question

ΔH is positive for this equilibrium between nitrogen and oxygen. How would you expect K_c to change with temperature?

Answer

If ΔH is positive, the reaction is endothermic, i.e. heat is required to move the equilibrium to the right. If the temperature of the reaction is raised, the system would have to absorb more energy. Le Chatelier's principle predicts that the equilibrium would respond to minimise this effect. The additional energy could be used to create more nitrogen oxide, i.e. move the equilibrium to the right.

Question

A mixture of hydrogen (concentration $10\,mol\,dm^{-3}$) and carbon dioxide ($90\,mol\,dm^{-3}$) was heated at $1200\,K$ so that steam and carbon monoxide were formed. At equilibrium, only $80.53\,mol\,dm^{-3}$ of carbon dioxide remained in the mixture. Calculate K_c for the reaction.

Answer

Equation is

$$H_2(g) + CO_2(g) \rightleftharpoons CO(g) + H_2O(g)$$

Examination of the equation shows that for every mole of carbon dioxide that is reduced, a mole of hydrogen reacts and a mole each of carbon monoxide and steam are formed. The changes involved are summarised below, with the calculated values for the concentrations (in $mol\,dm^{-3}$) in *italics*:

	$H_2(g)$	$CO_2(g)$	$CO(g)$	$H_2O(g)$
Start	10.00	90.00	0	0
At equilibrium	10.00−9.47	90.00−9.47		
	=0.53	=80.53	9.47	9.47
Changes	−9.47	−9.47	+9.47	+9.47

The equilibrium constant for the reaction is given by

$$K_c = \frac{[CO][H_2O]}{[H_2][CO_2]}$$

$$= \frac{9.47\,mol\,dm^{-3} \times 9.47\,mol\,dm^{-3}}{0.53\,mol\,dm^{-3} \times 80.53\,mol\,dm^{-3}}$$

$$= 2.10$$

We have now looked at the basic ideas behind chemical equilibrium, and with the Haber process we have seen how important the understanding of equilibria is. In chapter 5, we will use these ideas to understand how acids and bases behave.

SUMMARY

- A reversible reaction is a reaction that may proceed in either direction (forward or reverse), depending on the applied conditions.

- Dynamic equilibrium occurs when the rate for the forward reaction is equal to the rate of the reverse reaction, so that products are formed at the same rate as they are decomposed. The equilibrium is dynamic because it is maintained despite continual changes occurring between molecules.

- Le Chatelier's principle states that an equilibrium will shift so as to minimise the effect of a change in concentration, pressure or temperature.

- The equilibrium constant, K_c (for concentrations) or K_p (for pressures), is a constant that depends on both the type of reaction and the temperature. For example, in the reaction

  $$wA + xB = yC + zD$$

  K_c is given by

  $$K_c = \frac{[C]^y[D]^z}{[A]^w[B]^x}\,(mol\,dm^{-3})^{(y+z-w-x)}$$

  and K_p for reactions in the gas phase is given by

  $$K_p = \frac{\{p(C)\}^y\{p(D)\}^z}{\{p(A)\}^w\{p(B)\}^x}\,Pa^{(y+z-w-x)}$$

- The equilibrium constant is affected by a change in temperature. However, it is not affected by a change in concentration or pressure, or by the presence of a catalyst.

- A catalyst may accelerate the rate at which the reaction achieves equilibrium.

- The conditions used in the Haber and Contact processes are a compromise between ideal reaction conditions and the expense involved in producing those conditions. The key requirement is to produce the most yield for the least cost.

Acid–base equilibria

1 understand and use the Brønsted–Lowry theory of acids and bases;

2 explain the differences in behaviour between strong and weak acids and bases;

3 understand what is meant by the terms pH, K_a, pK_a and K_w, and use them in calculations;

4 calculate pH values and hydrogen-ion concentrations for acids and bases;

5 understand how to choose suitable indicators for acid–base titrations;

6 explain the changes in pH during acid–base titrations in terms of the strengths of acids and bases;

7 understand the use of pH meters and indicators in titrations and environmental monitoring;

8 understand how buffer solutions control pH, and describe their uses;

9 calculate the pH of buffer solutions;

10 understand and use the term *solubility product*, K_{sp};

11 calculate the solubility product from concentrations;

12 understand the common-ion effect.

that turns blue litmus red, and a base as something that tastes bitter, feels greasy and turns red litmus blue. Such statements have some validity, but are limited and arbitrary, and will also get you into trouble with the Health and Safety Inspectors! Nor do they help to explain what is going on when acids and bases take part in chemical reactions.

In some ways the Lewis definition of an acid and a base is superior. It may be used in all types of media, and so includes a greater range of substances and situations. However, the more limited Brønsted–Lowry definition works very well for the treatment of acid–base equilibria. It is particularly appropriate when considering the chemistry of aqueous solutions, so we will use it exclusively in this chapter. We will start with the formation of one of the most familiar acids of all – hydrochloric acid. It is made when hydrogen chloride, a gas, dissolves and reacts in water.

In aqueous solution, hydrogen chloride donates a proton to water to form the oxonium ion, $H_3O^+(aq)$, as shown in *figure 5.1*. However, for simplicity, we will refer to protons, H^+, rather than oxonium ions.

Definitions of acids and bases

In 1923, the Danish chemist J. N. Brønsted and the English chemist T. M. Lowry made the suggestion that an acid may be defined as a proton donor, and a base as a proton acceptor. A proton is a positive hydrogen ion, H^+. This is a long way from the first definitions you may have used for acids and bases (see *box 5A*).

Modern definitions are more precise than those which define an acid as something with a sour taste

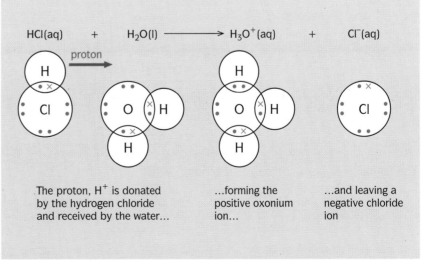

● **Figure 5.1** An acid is a proton donor. Hydrogen chloride is the acid in this reaction. A base is a proton receiver. Water is the base in this reaction.

Box 5A Acids and bases

Here are some definitions of acids and bases. (An alkali is a water-soluble base.)
Chemists tend to use the Brønsted–Lowry definition, as we will in this book.

Definition of acid	*Definition of base*	*Advantage of definition*
Tastes sharp or sour, like lemon	Tastes bitter, feels soapy or greasy	Is there any?
Turns purple cabbage juice red	Turns purple cabbage juice green or yellow	You can make your own indicator to test liquids
Turns blue litmus red	Turns red litmus blue	You can use test papers
Turns universal indicator red, orange or yellow	Turns universal indicator green, blue or purple	You can compare strengths of various acids and alkalis
Produces an excess of hydrogen ions, H^+, in aqueous solution (Arrhenius 1884)	Produces an excess of hydroxide ions, OH^-, in aqueous solution (Arrhenius 1884)	Enables acid–base reactions, e.g. neutralisation, to be explained as a reaction: $H^+(aq) + OH^-(aq) \longrightarrow H_2O(l)$
Donates protons during a chemical reaction (Brønsted and Lowry 1923)	Accepts protons during a chemical reaction (Brønsted and Lowry 1923)	Explains the role of water and why (for example) dilute H_2SO_4 is acidic but concentrated H_2SO_4 is not
Accepts an electron-pair during a reaction to form a covalent bond (Lewis 1923)	Donates an electron-pair during a reaction to form a covalent bond (Lewis 1923)	Incorporates a greater range of reactions than any other, including non-aqueous solutions and organic compounds

In contrast, a base will accept a proton to give the hydroxide ion, $OH^-(aq)$, as shown for ammonia in *figure 5.2*. Note that water behaves as a base in the hydrogen chloride solution, and as an acid in the ammonia solution.

In both cases we have omitted an important fact: the reactions should be written as equilibria. So for the first case we write

$$HCl(g) \overset{H_2O}{\rightleftharpoons} H^+(aq) + Cl^-(aq)$$

When we think about the forward reaction, $HCl(g)$ is an acid because it donates a proton, H^+. Water is a base because it receives this proton.

Now consider the reverse reaction:

$$H^+(aq) + Cl^-(aq) \overset{H_2O}{\rightleftharpoons} HCl(g)$$

The proton is donated to the chloride ion to form hydrogen chloride. (The oxonium ion, H_3O^+, a proton donor, is an acid.) At the same time the chloride ion, $Cl^-(aq)$, accepts a proton to become hydrogen

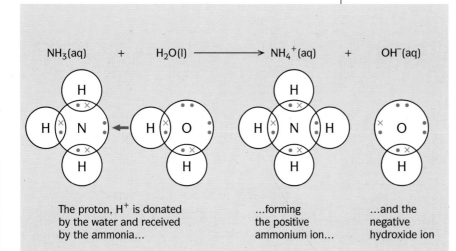

The proton, H^+ is donated by the water and received by the ammonia...

...forming the positive ammonium ion...

...and the negative hydroxide ion

● **Figure 5.2** Water is the proton donor (it is the acid); ammonia is the proton receiver (it is the base).

chloride. The chloride ion, a proton acceptor, is therefore a base. This can be summarised as shown:

$$HCl(g) + H_2O(l) \rightleftharpoons H_3O^+(aq) + Cl^-(aq)$$
B–L acid B–L base B–L acid B–L base

Look at the relationship between the species. The chlorine-containing species, $HCl(g)$ and $Cl^-(aq)$, form a pair. They are acid and base respectively, with the acid the richer in protons. We call this couple a **conjugate pair**.

SAQ 5.1

The oxygen-containing species also form a conjugate pair. Which is the conjugate acid in the pair? Which is the conjugate base? Is the conjugate acid richer in protons than its conjugate base?

SAQ 5.2

Examine the equilibrium

$$NH_3(g) + H_2O(l) \rightleftharpoons NH_4^+(aq) + OH^-(aq)$$

Which are the conjugate pairs of acid and base? Are the conjugate acids richer in protons than their conjugate bases?

How to spot an acid or a base

Know these definitions:

A Brønsted–Lowry acid is a proton donor, an H^+ giver

A Brønsted–Lowry base is a proton acceptor, an H^+ receiver

The Brønsted–Lowry definition applies to chemical changes in which protons, H^+, are transferred. Examine the change, and find the donors and receivers.

We shall now look at the following example. Which are the conjugate pairs of acid and base in this reaction?

$$NH_4^+(aq) + CO_3^{2-}(aq) \rightleftharpoons HCO_3^-(aq) + NH_3(aq)$$

We can see that the ammonium ion donates a proton to the carbonate ion, and forms ammonia. Thus the ammonium ion is an acid, and the ammonia is its conjugate base. The carbonate ion receives a proton, forming a hydrogencarbonate

ion. Thus the carbonate ion is a base, and the hydrogencarbonate ion is its conjugate acid. In both cases the conjugate acids are richer in protons than their conjugate bases. The equation can therefore be annotated as shown below:

conjugate pair
$$NH_4^+(aq) + CO_3^{2-}(aq) \rightleftharpoons HCO_3^-(aq) + NH_3(g)$$
B–L acid B–L base B–L acid B–L base
conjugate pair

SAQ 5.3

Use the Brønsted–Lowry definition of acid and base to identify the acids and bases in these equilibria and their conjugate bases and acids. Note that one of the reactions is not occurring in aqueous solution, a situation that could not be covered by earlier definitions of acid and base.

a $\qquad H_2SO_4(l) \overset{H_2O}{\rightleftharpoons} 2H^+(aq) + SO_4^{2-}(aq)$

b $\qquad C_6H_5COOH(aq) \overset{H_2O}{\rightleftharpoons} C_6H_5COO^-(aq) + H^+(aq)$

c $CH_3NH_2(aq) + H_2O(l) \rightleftharpoons CH_3NH_3^+(aq) + OH^-(aq)$

d $\qquad NH_3(g) + HCl(g) \rightleftharpoons NH_4^+Cl^-(s)$

The role of water

Water seems a familiar, almost benign substance, not one to be involved when acids react with bases, e.g. in the formation of common salt from sodium hydroxide and hydrochloric acid. It seems to sit on the sidelines:

$$NaOH(aq) + HCl(aq) \rightleftharpoons NaCl(aq) + H_2O(l)$$

Don't be misled. Water is not an innocent by-stander in acid–base reactions. Water plays a crucial part. It helps to understand this if you know more about pure water itself.

Water: facts and models

It is a fact that pure water conducts electricity, even if ever so slightly. It is quite unlike liquid helium, for example, or cyclohexane, which do not conduct electricity at all. Unlike these two substances, water contains ions that can carry charge – indeed pure water can be electrolysed by a direct current.

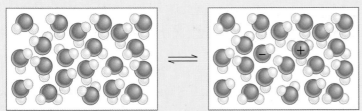

● **Figure 5.3** A proton is transferred from one water molecule to another, so that a positive ion, H_3O^+, is formed and a negative ion, OH^-, is left behind.

SAQ 5.4

Pure water is not a particularly good conductor. What does this tell you about the number of ions available for carrying a direct current?

We can imagine a model for the formation of ions from water molecules, in terms of proton transfer. Suppose every now and then one water molecule could react with another to form ions. It could be as shown in *figure 5.3*. Protons leave one molecule of water for another, ions are formed, and these ions can transfer electrons during electrolysis.

This reaction, sometimes called the auto-protolysis of water, can be summarised as

$$H_2O(l) \rightleftharpoons H^+(aq) + OH^-(aq)$$

SAQ 5.5

Experimental evidence tells us that the equilibrium constant, K_c, for this reaction is very, very small. At 298 K it is $1.80 \times 10^{-16}\,mol\,dm^{-3}$. What does this tell you about the relative proportions of water molecules, protons and hydroxide ions? Does this fit in with your knowledge of the electrical conductivity of pure water?

Base behaviour and neutralisation

Acids react with bases and are said to neutralise each other. It is interesting to look at what neutralises what. Consider what is present in two separate solutions of hydrochloric acid and sodium hydroxide.

■ In the acid $H^+(aq)$, $Cl^-(aq)$ and $H_2O(l)$
■ In the base $Na^+(aq)$, $OH^-(aq)$ and $H_2O(l)$

When this soup of ions is mixed, the protons and hydroxide ions meet and react as follows:

$$H^+(aq) + OH^-(aq) \rightleftharpoons H_2O(l);$$
$$\Delta H = \mp 57\,kJ\,mol^{-1}$$

As we saw above, the reaction favours the formation of water molecules – the equilibrium is well to the right. Hardly any of the protons and hydroxide ions remain. The vast majority neutralise each other to form water. This is what neutralisation is – the formation of water by the exothermic forward reaction shown above. The ions remaining, Na^+ and Cl^-, stay dissolved in that water – and would form salt crystals if the water was allowed to evaporate.

All reactions between acids and alkalis are like this. However, not all reagents release their protons and hydroxide ions in copious quantities as do the so-called strong acids like hydrochloric acid and the strong bases such as sodium hydroxide. We need to consider the relative strengths of acids and bases, and what this means for neutralisation.

Acids and bases of varying strength

Strong acids and bases are those which are totally ionised when dissolved in water. The strong acids include hydrogen halides and strong bases include the Group I metal hydroxides. Consider what happens when examples of these dissolve in water and then react.

For every mole of these solutes, a mole of each positive and negative ion is produced in solution:

$$LiOH(s) \xrightarrow{\text{water}} Li^+(aq) + OH^-(aq)$$

$$HCl(g) \xrightarrow{\text{water}} H^+(aq) + Cl^-(aq)$$

If a mole of protons mixes with a mole of hydroxide ions they combine to form virtually a mole of water molecules. Calculations show that for every thousand million water molecules formed by this reaction only one proton and hydroxide ion are uncombined.

Weak acids and weak bases do not ionise totally when they dissolve in water; in fact, they may hardly ionise at all. When it comes to donating protons, weak acids are very limited. Hydrogen sulphide is a good example. Hardly any protons are liberated when it reacts in water, so that the concentration of protons is low. In the reaction shown below, the equilibrium is very much to the left:

$$H_2S(g) \; \overset{H_2O(l)}{\rightleftharpoons} \; 2H^+(aq) + S^{2-}(aq)$$

Organic acids such as ethanoic acid (the sharp-tasting liquid in vinegar), and citric acid (the mouth-watering stuff of lemons) are typical weak acids. As proton donors go, they are pretty feeble. Weak bases are similarly feeble when it comes to accepting protons. They include the conjugate bases of strong acids, such as the sulphate and sulphite ions and (arguably) water itself.

As you will see, the relative strengths of acids and bases need to be known in order to monitor reactions between them. You need to understand the arithmetic behind measuring their relative strengths.

Introducing K_w, the ionic product of water

As shown already, pure water dissociates according to this equation:

$$H_2O(l) \rightleftharpoons H^+(aq) + OH^-(aq);$$
$$\Delta H = -57\,kJ\,mol^{-1}$$

The equilibrium constant for the dissociation of water molecules, K_c, is shown below:

$$K_c = \frac{[H^+][OH^-]}{[H_2O]} = 1.80 \times 10^{-16}\,mol\,dm^{-3} \text{ at } 298\,K$$

Thus

$$K_c[H_2O] = [H^+][OH^-]$$

The product, $[H^+][OH^-]$, is called the **ionic product of water**, K_w. We can calculate its value as shown below.

Since hardly any water dissociates, it is fair to assume that the concentration of water in the equilibrium is basically the same as what it was to start with. Since concentration is calculated in $mol\,dm^{-3}$, we need to know how many moles of

water there are in a decimetre cube. This amount is $55.6\,mol\,dm^{-3}$. Hence

$$\begin{aligned} K_w = [H^+][OH^-] &= K_c\,[H_2O] \\ &= 1.80 \times 10^{-16} \times 55.6\,mol^2\,dm^{-6} \\ &= 1.00 \times 10^{-14}\,mol^2\,dm^{-6} \end{aligned}$$

From the equation we can see that the concentration of protons equals the concentration of hydroxide ions. This means that the concentration of each species, $[H^+]$ and $[OH^-]$, is $1 \times 10^{-7}\,mol\,dm^{-3}$.

Introducing pH

The concentration of protons and hydroxide ions in pure water is clearly very small. Because it is awkward to fiddle about with tiny amounts like 1.0×10^{-7} (0.000 0001, a tenth of a millionth), chemists revert to using logarithmic scales. They do the same for large numbers too – see *box 5B*.

Chemists define pH as $-\log[H_3O^+]$, i.e. the negative logarithm to the base ten of the concentration of the oxonium ion. (The negative part helps us to cope with very small numbers, actually negative powers of ten). Historically, chemists referred to hydrogen ions, H^+, instead of oxonium ions, which is just as well; pH_3O is much too clumsy! Now you can appreciate why a neutral aqueous solution has a pH of 7:

$$pH = -\log_{10}[H^+]$$

With an electronic calculator, the calculation is as follows:

- Step 1: Enter the concentration 10^{-7} or 0.000 0001
- Step 2: Press the log button   Ans: -7
- Step 3: Change the sign from $-$ to $+$ Ans: $+7$

SAQ 5.6

Use the same process to calculate the pH of these solutions:

a An aqueous solution with $[H^+] = 3 \times 10^{-4}\,mol\,dm^{-3}$ (e.g. a cola drink).

b An aqueous solution with $[H^+] = 1 \times 10^{-2}\,mol\,dm^{-3}$ (stomach contents!).

c An aqueous solution with $[H^+] = 4 \times 10^{-8}\,mol\,dm^{-3}$ (blood).

You can use the reverse process to calculate the concentration of protons. For example, calculate the concentration of protons in an aqueous solution with pH = 3.2.

- Step 1: Enter the value   3.2
- Step 2: Change the sign   −3.2
- Step 3: Press the inverse log button or press the 10^x button

                                         0.00063 or 6.3×10^{-4}

- Step 4: Remember the units: $6.3 \times 10^{-4} \, \text{mol} \, \text{dm}^{-3}$

The pH values of some aqueous solutions with which you might be familiar are shown in *table 5.2*.

Calculating the pH of strong acids and strong bases

Strong acids dissociate completely. This means that we know, from the initial concentration of the strong acid, just how many protons are present in a solution. If one mole of a monobasic acid, which has one replaceable proton, such as hydrochloric acid is present in a decimetre cube of solution, then the concentration of protons is $1 \, \text{mol} \, \text{dm}^{-3}$. You can see this from the equation:

$$\underset{\substack{\\ 1\,\text{mol}}}{\text{HCl(g)}} \quad \overset{\text{H}_2\text{O(l)}}{\rightleftharpoons} \quad \underset{\substack{\\ 1\,\text{mol}}}{\text{H}^+\text{(aq)}} + \underset{\substack{\\ 1\,\text{mol}}}{\text{Cl}^-\text{(aq)}}$$

Box 5B Little numbers, large numbers and logs

Chemists deal with little and large. Miniscule molecules of water in enormous numbers are found in a sip of lemonade. To cope with this number range, we use powers of ten, as shown below:

Number of molecules of water in a sip of lemonade	300 000 000 000 000 000 000 000	3×10^{23}
Distance between the atoms in a molecule of water	0.000 000 000 111 metres	1.11×10^{-10} m

Other numbers that chemists might come across include the mass of the Earth (5.97×10^{24} kg) and the mass of a hydrogen atom (1.67×10^{-27} kg).

Ten to the power of 3 (10^3 or 1000) is ten times bigger than ten to the power of 2 (10^2 or 100). Powers of ten represent tenfold jumps in size and are called logarithms. Because we count in tens (unlike computers, which count in twos), we call these powers 'logarithms to the base ten', and write them as $\log_{10}$.

Table 5.1 shows how $\log_{10}$ is used to represent the range of numbers we might use.

Example	*Number*		*Log$_{10}$*
Molecules of ozone in $1\,\text{cm}^3$ of air on a good day	100 000 000 000 000	$= 10^{14}$	14.0
Speed of light in metres per second	300 000 000	$= 3 \times 10^8$	8.5
Solubility of $Ca(OH)_2$ in water in moles per 100 g	0.00153	$= 1.53 \times 10^{-3}$	−2.8
Concentration of protons in pure water at 298 K in moles per decimetre cube	0.0000001	$= 1 \times 10^{-7}$	−7.0
Concentration of protons in $0.1\,\text{mol}\,\text{dm}^{-3}$ NaOH(aq) in moles per decimetre cube	0.000 000 000 0001	$= 1 \times 10^{-13}$	−13.0

● **Table 5.1** You will come across the term 'negative log' or '−$\log_{10}$'. This is not to complicate matters. It is simply a way of getting rid of the minus sign of the log of a small number. If $\log_{10}(X) = -3$, then $-\log_{10}(X) = -1 \times -3 = 3$

Solution	pH
hydrochloric acid ($1 \, mol \, dm^{-3}$)	0.0
hydrochloric acid ($0.1 \, mol \, dm^{-3}$)	1.0
hydrochloric acid ($0.01 \, mol \, dm^{-3}$)	2.0
stomach 'juices' (contain HCl(aq))	1.0–1.5
lemon juice	2.3
vinegar	3
coffee	around 5
rain-water (normal)	5.7
saliva	6.3–6.8
urine	6.0–7.4
fresh milk	around 6.5
pure water	7.0
blood	7.4
pancreatic juices	7.1–8.2
sea-water	around 8.5
baking soda in water	around 9
milk of magnesia	10
soapy water (cheap soap!)	11
bench sodium hydroxide ($0.1 \, mol \, dm^{-3}$)	13
bench sodium hydroxide ($1 \, mol \, dm^{-3}$)	14

● **Table 5.2** pH values of some familiar aqueous solutions

The pH of a $1 \, mol \, dm^{-3}$ solution of hydrochloric acid is therefore $-\log_{10}[H^+] = -\log_{10}[1.0]$, i.e. zero. The situation is slightly different with a strong dibasic acid, which has two replaceable protons, such as sulphuric acid. Each mole of dibasic acid produces two moles of protons:

$$H_2SO_4(g) \underset{}{\overset{H_2O(l)}{\rightleftharpoons}} 2H^+(aq) + SO_4^{2-}(aq)$$
$$\text{1 mol} \qquad \text{2 mol} \qquad \text{1 mol}$$

The pH of an aqueous solution containing $1 \, mol \, dm^{-3}$ of sulphuric acid is calculated from the data in the equation above as shown:

$$H_2SO_4(g) \underset{}{\overset{H_2O(l)}{\rightleftharpoons}} 2H^+(aq) + SO_4^{2-}(aq)$$
$$\text{1 mol} \qquad \text{2 mol} \qquad \text{1 mol}$$

$$pH = -\log_{10}[H^+] = -\log_{10}[2] = -0.3$$

Strong bases also produce stoichiometric amounts of protons in solution, although it is much less obvious. We tend to think of strong bases as producers of hydroxide ions, but of course there are protons present too – only in very small quantities. Follow the calculation below, for the pH of a $0.05 \, mol \, dm^{-3}$ solution of sodium hydroxide.

Sodium hydroxide ionises completely:

$$NaOH(s) \overset{water}{\longrightarrow} Na^+(aq) + OH^-(aq)$$
$$\text{1 mol} \qquad \text{1 mol} \qquad \text{1 mol}$$
$$\text{0.05 mol} \qquad \text{0.05 mol} \qquad \text{0.05 mol}$$

The concentration of hydroxide ions in a $0.05 \, mol \, dm^{-3}$ NaOH solution is clearly $0.05 \, mol \, dm^{-3}$. Now the ionic product of water, K_w, is constant and equals $1 \times 10^{-14} \, mol \, dm^{-3}$. This means we can write

$$K_w = [H^+][OH^-] = 1 \times 10^{-14} \, mol^2 \, dm^{-6}$$

so

$$[H^+] = \frac{1 \times 10^{-14} \, mol^2 \, dm^{-6}}{[OH^-] \, mol \, dm^{-3}} = \frac{1 \times 10^{-14}}{0.05} \, mol \, dm^{-3}$$
$$= 2 \times 10^{-13} \, mol \, dm^{-3}$$

so

$$pH = -\log_{10}[H^+] = -\log_{10}(2 \times 10^{-13}) = 12.7$$

There is a quicker way of getting the same answer: find $-\log_{10}[OH^-]$ and subtract it from 14.

SAQ 5.7

Find the pH of the following strong acids and strong bases given that $K_w = 1.0 \times 10^{-14} \, mol^2 \, dm^{-6}$ at 298 K.

a $1 \, mol \, dm^{-3}$ nitric acid, HNO_3(aq).

b $0.5 \, mol \, dm^{-3}$ nitric acid, HNO_3(aq).

c $0.02 \, mol \, dm^{-3}$ sulphuric acid, H_2SO_4 (aq).

d An aqueous solution containing 3 g of hydrogen chloride, HCl, per dm^3.

e A $0.001 \, mol \, dm^{-3}$ potassium hydroxide solution, KOH(aq).

f An aqueous solution containing 0.2 g of sodium hydroxide, NaOH, per dm^3.

Ionic equilibria: the definition of K_a and pK_a

The following single equation summarises all strong acid–strong base neutralisations:

$$H^+(aq) + OH^-(aq) \rightleftharpoons H_2O(l);$$
$$\Delta H = \mp 57 \, kJ \, mol^{-1}$$

In keeping with this, the same enthalpy change of reaction is observed whatever strong acid–strong base combination is involved (provided the solution is sufficiently dilute that the other ions do not interact), so that the reaction above goes to completion.

Most acids are weak. They do not react completely with water. A good example is ethanoic acid, of which vinegar is a dilute solution. Here the ethanoic acid will donate a proton to water, so it is indeed an acid, but the backward reaction, the acceptance of a proton by the ethanoate anion, must also be taken into account. When the two reactions are proceeding at the same rate, this equilibrium is set up:

$$CH_3COOH(aq) \rightleftharpoons CH_3COO^-(aq) + H^+(aq)$$

The equilibrium constant K_c can now be written:

$$K_c = \frac{[CH_3COO^-][H^+]}{[CH_3COOH]} \, mol \, dm^{-3}$$

This constant is usually written as K_a, the **acid dissociation constant**, and at 298 K for ethanoic acid its value is $1.7 \times 10^{-5} \, mol \, dm^{-3}$. Its value gives us a feel for the strength of the acid, and of course the extent to which it ionises in water. This can be seen in the general equation below:

$$HA(aq) \rightleftharpoons A^-(aq) + H^+(aq)$$

so

$$K_a = \frac{[A^-][H^+]}{[HA]} \, mol \, dm^{-3}$$

If the acid dissociates to a large extent, $[A^-]$ and $[H^+]$ are relatively large, and $[HA]$ is smaller. Both effects would make K_a comparatively big. You can see this in *table 5.3*. Yet again we can be dealing with a large range of values, some of them very small. Just as pH was invented for oxonium-ion concentration, pK_a has been invented to deal with the dissociation of acids.

$$pK_a = -\log_{10}[K_a]$$

SAQ 5.8

Look at *table 5.3*. Work out which species are Brønsted–Lowry acids, and which are conjugate bases.

Calculating the percentage ionisation of a weak acid

Consider the percentage ionisation for a $0.05 \, mol \, dm^{-3}$ solution of ethanoic acid. This is the equation for the dissociation:

$$CH_3COOH(aq) \rightleftharpoons CH_3COO^-(aq) + H^+(aq)$$

Assume that x moles of ethanoic acid ionise. This helps us to create a 'before-and-after' scenario as shown:

	$CH_3COOH(aq) \rightleftharpoons$	$CH_3COO^-(aq) +$	$H^+(aq)$
Before	0.05 moles	0 moles	0 moles
After	$(0.05 - x)$ moles	x moles	x moles

Acid or ion	Equilibrium in aqueous solution	K_a	pK_a
nitric	$HNO_3 \rightleftharpoons H^+ + NO_3^-$	About 40	-1.4
sulphurous	$H_2SO_3 \rightleftharpoons H^+ + HSO_3^-$	1.5×10^{-2}	1.8
hydrated Fe^{3+} ion	$Fe(H_2O)_6^{3+} \rightleftharpoons H^+ + Fe(H_2O)_5(OH)^{2+}$	6.0×10^{-3}	2.2
hydrofluoric	$HF \rightleftharpoons H^+ + F^-$	5.6×10^{-4}	3.3
nitrous	$HNO_2 \rightleftharpoons H^+ + NO_2^-$	4.7×10^{-4}	3.3
methanoic	$HCOOH \rightleftharpoons H^+ + HCOO^-$	1.6×10^{-4}	3.8
benzoic	$C_6H_5COOH \rightleftharpoons H^+ + C_6H_5COO^-$	6.3×10^{-5}	4.2
ethanoic	$CH_3COOH \rightleftharpoons H^+ + CH_3COO^-$	1.7×10^{-5}	4.8
propanoic	$CH_3CH_2COOH \rightleftharpoons H^+ + CH_3CH_2COO^-$	1.3×10^{-5}	4.9
hydrated Al^{3+} ion	$Al(H_2O)_6^{3+} \rightleftharpoons H^+ + Al(H_2O)_5(OH)^{2+}$	1.0×10^{-5}	5.0
carbonic	$CO_2 + H_2O \rightleftharpoons H^+ + HCO_3^-$	4.5×10^{-7}	6.4
silicic	$SiO_2 + H_2O \rightleftharpoons H^+ + HSiO_3^-$	1.3×10^{-10}	9.9
hydrogencarbonate ion	$HCO_3^- \rightleftharpoons H^+ + CO_3^{2-}$	4.8×10^{-11}	10.3
hydrogensilicate ion	$HSiO_3^- \rightleftharpoons H^+ + SiO_3^{2-}$	1.3×10^{-12}	11.9
water	$H_2O \rightleftharpoons H^+ + OH^-$	1.0×10^{-14}	14.0

● **Table 5.3** Acid dissociation constants, K_a, for a range of acids, for aqueous solutions in the region of $0.0–0.01 \, mol \, dm^{-3}$

The next thing to do is to write the formula for K_a:

$$K_a = \frac{[CH_3COO^-][H^+]}{[CH_3COOH]} = 1.7 \times 10^{-5} \, mol \, dm^{-3}$$

We can now substitute the 'after' concentrations in this equation:

$$K_a = \frac{(x \, mol \, dm^{-3})(x \, mol \, dm^{-3})}{(0.05 - x) \, mol \, dm^{-3}}$$

$$= 1.7 \times 10^{-5} \, mol \, dm^{-3}$$

So

$$x^2 = 1.7 \times 10^{-5} \times (0.05 - x)$$

This gives a quadratic equation in x, which could be solved using a general formula. However, we can make a justifiable approximation to avoid doing this. We assume that the dissociation of ethanoic acid is so slight that essentially we can take the final concentration after dissociation as the same as that before. In other words, in the term $(0.05 - x)$, x is so small that we can assume the term equals 0.05 itself. This type of approximation is often made in this kind of calculation, but it's best at the end, before laying down your pencil with a sigh of relief, to just check that it's valid. A fiddle has got be an acceptable fiddle! As shown in the final part of the calculation, we find that the percentage ionisation is 1.8%. Since dissociation constants are usually accurate to about 5%, it can be seen that our approximation in this case is a reasonable one.

Assuming $(0.05 - x) = 0.05$ because x is very small in a weak acid, we get

$$x^2 = 1.7 \times 10^{-5} \times 0.05 = 8.5 \times 10^{-7} = 85 \times 10^{-8}$$

$$x = \sqrt{85 \times 10^{-8}} = 9.2 \times 10^{-4}$$

$$= 9.2 \times 10^{-4} \, mol \, dm^{-3}$$

So the percentage ionisation of ethanoic acid is

$$\frac{9.2 \times 10^{-4} \, mol \, dm^{-3}}{0.05 \, mol \, dm^{-3}} \times 100\% = 1.8\%$$

Solving the full quadratic equation without making any approximations gives $x = 9.1 \times 10^{-4} \, mol \, dm^{-3}$ and (again) a percentage ionisation of 1.8%. In this case the fiddle is perfectly acceptable!

Calculating the pH of weak acids

Now we can calculate the pH of a $0.05 \, mol \, dm^{-3}$ solution of ethanoic acid. Look again at the equation for the dissociation. The concentration of protons from the acid is x. If we assume that water itself provides virtually no protons, then our solution contains $9.2 \times 10^{-4} \, mol$ of protons per dm^3. Since $pH = -log_{10}[H^+]$, then the pH of the ethanoic acid = 3.0.

SAQ 5.9

Using the data from *table 5.3* work out the following:

a The percentage ionisation and pH of a solution containing $0.02 \, mol \, dm^{-3}$ of benzoic acid in water.

b The pH of an aqueous solution containing $0.01 \, mol \, dm^{-3}$ of aluminium ions.

c The pH of a solution of $0.1 \, mol \, dm^{-3}$ methanoic acid in water.

SAQ 5.10

Explain with reference to *table 5.3* why dissolving iron(III) chloride in water produces an acidic solution.

Ionic equilibria: the definition of pK_b

We can also distinguish between strong bases and weak bases. A strong base is either an ionic compound containing the hydroxide anion, for example sodium hydroxide, or an ion or molecule that is completely protonated by water to yield a significant amount of hydroxide ion. The hydride anion, H^-, falls into this category, as shown in the equations below. Group I metals form hydrides that yield these anions in aqueous solution. For example:

$$NaH(s) \xrightarrow{H_2O} Na^+(aq) + H^-(aq)$$

$$H^-(aq) + H_2O(l) \rightleftharpoons H_2(g) + OH^-(aq)$$

water protonates (donates a proton to) the hydride ion

SAQ 5.11

Which are the Brønsted–Lowry acids and bases in this protonation reaction?

Base	Equilibrium in aqueous solution	K_b	pK_b
lead hydroxide	$Pb(OH)_2 \rightleftharpoons PbOH^+ + OH^-$	9.6×10^{-4}	3.0
silver hydroxide	$AgOH \rightleftharpoons Ag^+ + OH^-$	1.1×10^{-4}	4.0
ammonia	$NH_3 + H_2O \rightleftharpoons NH_4^+ + OH^-$	1.8×10^{-5}	4.8
hydroxylamine (at 293 K)	$NH_2OH + H_2O \rightleftharpoons NH_3OH^+ + OH^-$	1.1×10^{-8}	8.0

● **Table 5.4** Base dissociation constants, K_b for a range of bases, for aqueous solutions in the region of 0.0–$0.01\,mol\,dm^{-3}$ at 298 K

A weak base is incompletely protonated by water, so an equilibrium of the kind shown below is set up, enabling definition of K_b by analogy with the definition of K_a:

$$B(aq) + H_2O(l) \rightleftharpoons BH^+(aq) + OH^-(aq)$$

$$K_c = \frac{[BH^+][OH^-]}{[B][H_2O]}$$

Since in all cases we shall be considering very dilute solutions, so that there is no inter-ionic influences, the concentration of water, $[H_2O]$, will be a constant. The concentration of water is so large, and so little of it dissociates, that to all intents and purposes it stays the same. This means that we can cross-multiply it with K_c to create another constant, K_b, the **base dissociation constant**. So

$$K_c[H_2O] = K_b = \frac{[BH^+][OH^-]}{[B]}$$

and

$$pK_b = -\log_{10}K_b$$

In some cases, the equation will be

$$BOH \rightleftharpoons B^+ + OH^-$$

K_c will be the same as K_b in these cases.

Some base dissociation constants are listed in *table 5.4*.

SAQ 5.12

For each of the equilibria in *table 5.4*, work out which species is a Brønsted–Lowry base, and which is its conjugate acid.

Constant relationships for things to come

Let us look at the relationships between K_a and K_b and their counterparts pK_a and pK_b. These will be useful when you look at buffer solutions.

For any Brønsted–Lowry acid, HA, there is an equilibrium in aqueous solution:

$$\underset{\text{B–L acid}}{HA(aq)} \rightleftharpoons H^+(aq) + \underset{\text{conjugate base}}{A^-(aq)}$$

so for this acid

$$K_a = \frac{[H^+][A^-]}{[HA]}$$

For the acid's conjugate base, A^-, there is an equilibrium in aqueous solution:

$$\underset{\text{conjugate base}}{A^-(aq)} + H_2O \rightleftharpoons \underset{\text{B–L acid}}{HA(aq)} + OH^-(aq)$$

so for this base

$$K_b = \frac{[HA][OH^-]}{[A^-]}$$

Multiplying K_a by K_b we have

$$K_a \times K_b = \frac{[H^+][A^-]}{[HA]} \times \frac{[HA][OH^-]}{[A^-]}$$

$$= [H^+][OH^-] = K_w$$

so

$$K_a \times K_b = 1 \times 10^{-14}\,mol^2\,dm^{-6}$$

If we multiply by both sides of this equation by -1 and take logarithms we find that

$$pK_a + pK_b = 14$$

so

$$pK_a = 14 - pK_b$$

and

$$pK_b = 14 - pK_a$$

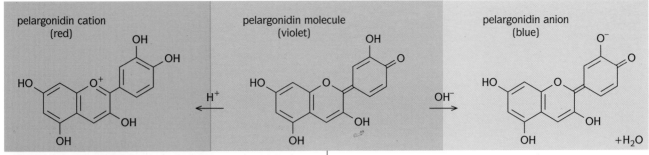

pelargonidin cation
(red)

pelargonidin molecule
(violet)

pelargonidin anion
(blue)

H^+ OH^-

$+H_2O$

● *Figure 5.4* The red petals of geraniums contain the dye pelargonidin. Protons and hydroxide ions can tweak its molecular structure to produce different colours.

Measuring pH

Many dyes are susceptible to acids and alkalis. Their molecular structure can be modified by changes in concentration so that they change colour (*figure 5.4*).

pH affects the colour of some dyes in quite dramatic ways. The dyes are used in the laboratory, sometimes as mixtures, to monitor the pH of chemical changes; when used in this way, they are called **indicators.** They usually change over a pH range of between 1 and 2 'units', with a recognised end-point somewhere in the middle. The pH of the end-point is given as pK_{ind} ('ind' stands for 'indicator'). The end-point is the point where the indicator is most clearly seen to be between the two extremes of its colour.

For example, bromothymol blue is yellow in acidic solutions and blue in alkaline solutions. The colour-change range varies from pH 6.0 to pH 7.6 and the end-point occurs when the pH is 7.0. The colours, ranges and end-points vary considerably, as can be seen in *table 5.5*. For example, phenolphthalein is colourless in solutions with pH less than 8.2 and does not reach its final red colour until the pH is 10. Protons and hydroxide ions have a considerable effect on the molecular structure as shown in *figure 5.5*.

Universal indicator is actually a choice mixture of dyes whose combined colours can create a range of hues, each corresponding to a pH unit – or even fraction of a unit. Indicators can be designed to incorporate a wide pH range, e.g. 1–11, or for specific tasks a smaller range, e.g. pH 4–6 in intervals of 0.2 of a pH 'unit'.

Name of dye	Colour at low pH	pH range	End-point (pK$_{ind}$)	Colour at higher pH
Methyl violet	yellow	0.0–1.6	0.8	blue
Methyl yellow	red	2.9–4.0	3.5	yellow
Methyl orange	red	3.2–4.4	3.7	yellow
Bromophenol blue	yellow	2.8–4.6	4.0	blue
Bromocresol green	yellow	3.8–5.4	4.7	blue
Methyl red	red	4.2–6.3	5.1	yellow
Bromothymol blue	yellow	6.0–7.6	7.0	blue
Phenolphthalein	colourless	8.2–10.0	9.3	pink/violet
Alizarin yellow	yellow	10.1–13.0	12.5	orange/red

● *Table 5.5* Some of the chemical indicators used to monitor pH, with their pH ranges of use and pH of end-point (pK$_{ind}$)

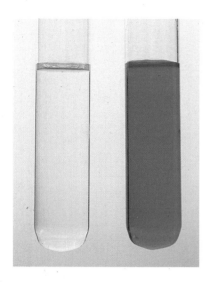

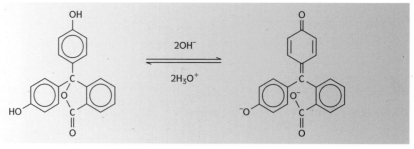

● **Figure 5.5** Colour change in phenolphthalein. At a pH of less than 8.2, the molecular structure isolates three benzene rings, each with its own delocalised electrons in a different plane from the other two. In more alkaline solutions, the structure changes: an ion is formed (a flat ion!) and delocalised electrons extend over virtually the entire structure. This extended electron system absorbs most, but not all, of the light in the visible spectrum, so that the solution is pink.

Any measurement made using dyes must be subjective and far from accurate. There can also be problems with coloured solutions, e.g. beer (where pH measurement is routine). For the accurate measurements required for research, particularly in biological and biochemical areas, pH measurement is done electrically. Great accuracy can be achieved with modern pH meters.

Acids with alkalis: monitoring change

Measuring the concentration of acid and alkaline solutions is a routine task. A traditional method involves titration, i.e. measuring just how much of a reagent of known concentration is needed to react with all of another. *Figure 5.6* shows a familiar example, the titration of a strong acid against a strong base. Bear in mind that neutralisation means the reaction between equal amounts of protons and hydroxide ions to form water (page 76).

Strong acids with strong bases

Figure 5.6 shows a strong acid being titrated 'against' a strong base. The acid is delivered slowly from the burette into the alkali in the

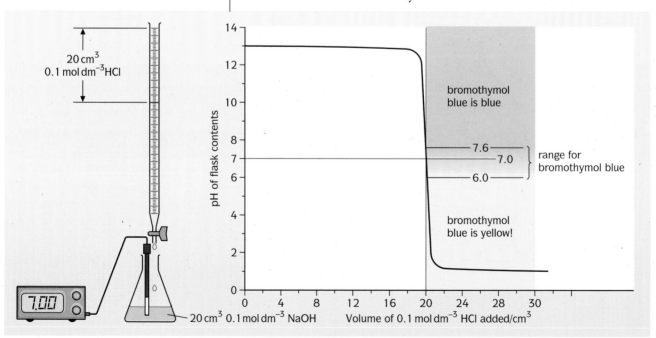

● **Figure 5.6** A strong acid–strong base titration produces a characteristic graph.

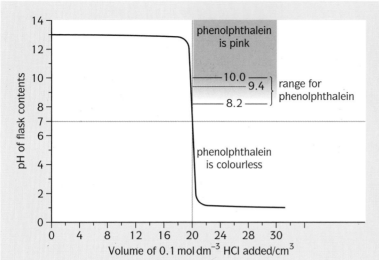

● *Figure 5.7* A strong acid–strong base titration with phenolphthalein as the indicator.

flask, with constant stirring. The pH of the mixture is monitored using a pH meter, and values recorded manually or by a data logger. The graph shows how the pH changes as drop after drop is added. Note the sharp fall in the graph. In this region, tiny additional amounts of protons from the acid have a drastic effect on pH. The midpoint of this steep slope corresponds to a pH of 7. An indicator such as bromothymol blue, which changes from blue to yellow over the range 6.0–7.6, would register this change. Note, however, that the slope is steep over the range pH = 3.5 to pH = 10.5. Other indicators would

also mark this sudden change. Phenolphthalein, effective in the pH range 8.2 to 10.0, could also be used (*figure 5.7*).

SAQ 5.13

Use *table 5.5* to identify those indicators which could used for a strong acid–strong base titration like this, and those which could not.

Strong acids with weak bases

A strong acid such as $0.1\,mol\,dm^{-3}$ nitric acid reacts with a weak base like ammonium hydroxide as shown in *figure 5.8*. Which part of the graph corresponds to the graph in *figure 5.7*? Methyl orange would be a suitable indicator, as the sudden decrease of pH occurs in the range in which methyl orange changes colour, i.e. 3.2–4.4.

SAQ 5.14

Use *table 5.5* to find those indicators which could be used for the above, and those which could not.

Weak acids with strong bases

The change in pH for the reaction of a weak acid such as benzoic acid with a strong base such as potassium hydroxide is shown in *figure 5.9*.

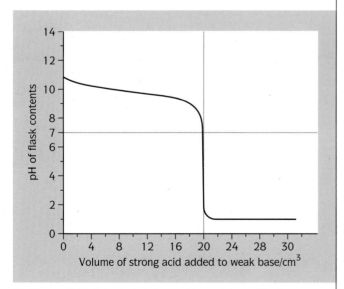

● *Figure 5.8* A typical strong acid–weak base titration.

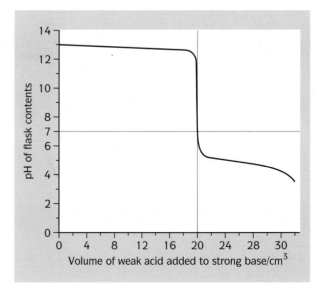

● *Figure 5.9* A typical weak acid–strong base titration.

SAQ 5.15

Compare *figure 5.9* to *figures 5.7* and *5.8*, noticing similarities and differences. Phenolphthalein, with its pK_{ind} at 9.3, is a suitable indicator for the end-point in *figure 5.9*. Why would methyl orange be unsuitable?

Weak acids with weak bases

As *figure 5.10* shows, there is no significant pH range in which the addition of a small amount of one reagent produces a sharp change. In circumstances like this, none of the indicators in *table 5.5* would be effective. In the example shown, bromothymol blue would start to change colour when $19.5\,cm^3$ of acid had been added, and would finish changing after another $1\,cm^3$ had been added. Such a large range is unacceptable in situations when an accuracy of $0.02\,cm^3$ is reasonable.

SAQ 5.16

Suggest a suitable indicator to find the end-points of the reactions between:

a $0.05\,mol\,dm^{-3}$ nitric acid and silver hydroxide;

b $2\,mol\,dm^{-3}$ sodium hydroxide solution and $1\,mol\,dm^{-3}$ sulphuric acid;

c $0.005\,mol\,dm^{-3}$ potassium hydroxide and aspirin (2-ethanoyloxybenzoic acid), which has an equilibrium constant of $3 \times 10^{-4}\,mol\,dm^{-3}$.

Salts as acids and bases

Sodium ethanoate, the sodium salt of a weak acid, is highly soluble in water and dissociates completely as shown:

$$CH_3COONa(s) \rightleftharpoons CH_3COO^-(aq) + Na^+(aq)$$

Once in solution, the ethanoate ion can react with water in the following equilibrium:

$$CH_3COO^-(aq) + H_2O(l)$$
$$\rightleftharpoons CH_3COOH(aq) + OH^-(aq)$$

Since ethanoic acid is a weak acid, the equilibrium is very much to the right. The concentration of hydroxyl ions is therefore higher than that of protons, and the salt solution is slightly alkaline.

The reverse effect is observed with the salt of a weak base and a strong acid, e.g. ammonium hydrogensulphate. This dissociates in water:

$$NH_4HSO_4(s) \rightleftharpoons NH_4^+(aq) + HSO_4^-(aq)$$

The ammonium ions then dissociate in the following equilibrium:

$$NH_4^+(aq) \rightleftharpoons NH_3(aq) + H^+(aq)$$

Again the equilibrium is very much to the right. The concentration of protons is therefore much higher than that of hydroxyl ions, and the salt solution is acidic. *Table 5.6* gives a rule-of-thumb guide to the pH of salts.

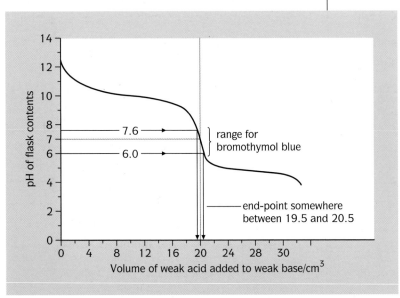

● **Figure 5.10** A typical weak acid–weak base titration.

Salt pH	Combination needed to produce salt
nearly 7	strong acid with strong base
less than 7	strong acid with weak base
greater than 7	weak acid with strong base

● **Table 5.6** Guide to the pH of salts

Buffer solutions

In *table 5.2* the pH values of a number of commonly occurring solutions were given. Often it does not matter if these pH values vary slightly, but for biological solutions (stomach contents and saliva, for example), and for many industrial processes, it is important to maintain a constant pH. It can be vital. If your blood pH increases or decreases by 0.5, you will lose consciousness and drift into a coma. Your blood has to have some sort of control system to cope with increase in proton or hydroxide ion concentration. It has to have a buffer – something to soak up any increase in the proton or hydroxyl ion concentrations.

A **buffer solution** is one that can maintain a reasonably constant pH, even when moderate amounts of acid or base are added to it. However, no buffer solution can cope with an excessive supply of acid or alkali.

A solution of sodium ethanoate in ethanoic acid is just such a solution. It operates because the equilibria shown below respond to increases in proton or hydroxide ion concentration in such a way as to minimise the increase – another practical application of Le Chatelier's principle.

Note that ethanoic acid and sodium ethanoate must both be present for the buffer solution to be effective. The sodium ethanoate dissociates completely to produce ethanoate ions:

$$CH_3COONa(aq) \longrightarrow CH_3COO^-(aq) + Na^+(aq)$$

This complete dissociation influences the dissociation of ethanoic acid, which reaches an equilibrium:

$$CH_3COOH(aq) \rightleftharpoons H^+(aq) + CH_3COO^-(aq)$$

The result is that there are large reservoirs of the acid, CH_3COOH, and its conjugate base, CH_3COO^-. This means that the following equilibria are brought into balance:

$$CH_3COO^-(aq) + H^+(aq) \rightleftharpoons CH_3COOH(aq)$$
(mainly from sodium ethanoate) $\qquad\qquad$ *(5.1)*

$$CH_3COOH(aq) + OH^-(aq)$$
$$\rightleftharpoons CH_3COO^-(aq) + H_2O(l) \qquad (5.2)$$

An increase in proton concentration would rapidly lower the pH of water. However, in this buffer solution it shifts the equilibrium in *equation 5.1* to the right. Protons are transferred to the ethanoate ions (of which there are plenty) so that ethanoic acid is formed. A moderate input of protons therefore has a marginal effect on the overall pH.

The effect of an alkali, which in water would rapidly increase the pH, is minimised in a similar way. The equilibrium in *equation 5.2* shifts to the right as hydroxide ions remove protons from ethanoic acid molecules to form ethanoate ions and water.

You may come across alternative explanations for the way in which this buffer solution copes with an increase of hydroxide ions. The explanation suggests that the hydroxide ions first neutralise any protons present, which are then replaced by the dissociation of more ethanoic acid. The fact is that we don't know which mechanism actually operates – so keep it simple. Remember the two components – the weak acid, which counters the addition of hydroxide ions, and the salt of the weak acid (itself alkaline in solution), which counters the addition of protons.

Proteins, 'bicarb' and pH control

You are probably familiar with the idea of blood as an oxygen carrier. Oxygen from the air diffuses into your bloodstream in the lungs, and reacts with haemoglobin. This 'organo-metallic' compound, the first protein ever to be obtained as a crystalline solid, contains iron – hence its red colour. It reacts with oxygen as shown:

haemoglobin + dissolved oxygen
$\qquad \rightleftharpoons$ oxyhaemoglobin

This reaction is easily reversed in tissues all over the body, releasing oxygen for the energy-generating process called aerobic respiration. For example, glucose oxidises in an exothermic reaction, producing water, carbon dioxide and heat. The equation below is a gross over-simplification of the many reactions that it summarises.

$$C_6H_{12}O_6(aq) + 6O_2(aq)$$
$$\longrightarrow 6CO_2(aq) + 6H_2O(aq);$$
$$\Delta H = -2820\,kJ\,mol^{-1}$$

Your blood is now left with a waste-disposal problem, which is potentially poisonous. The problem, and part of the solution, lies in the equation below. The rates of both the forward and backward reactions in the equilibrium are rapid, thanks to the enzyme carbonic anhydrase.

$$H_2O(aq) + CO_2(aq) \overset{\text{carbonic anhydrase}}{\rightleftharpoons} H^+(aq) + HCO_3^-(aq)$$

The generation of protons, if unchecked, would lead to a lowering of blood pH and you would slip into a coma. Your blood needs a buffer.

In fact, it has at least *three*, the most important by far being the buffering action of hydrogencarbonate ion, $HCO_3^-(aq)$. Haemoglobin and plasma, both proteins, also act as buffers, but are much less effective.

Protons in the blood are mopped up by hydrogencarbonate ions, the equation being the one above in which the equilibrium is well to the left. The carbon dioxide produced is carried to the lungs and breathed out. Lung infections that inhibit breathing can hinder this extraction process, leading to acidosis – i.e. decrease in blood pH.

The chemistry of pH control in the body is more complex than this section suggests, involving many other ions, particularly when acidosis is severe. The kidneys also play a crucial part. Understanding pH control is vital when treating certain diseases, e.g. coronary thrombosis. Anaesthetists constantly monitor blood pH in long operations that involve heart–lung machines, and may inject controlled amounts of sodium hydrogencarbonate – 'bicarb' – to cater for a pH fall.

Making buffer solutions of desired pH

To make up a buffer solution at a given pH, you need a weak acid with a pK_a value of around the required pH and the salt of this acid (its conjugate base). A buffer solution of pH about 4 could be made from methanoic acid, HCOOH ($pK_a = 3.8$), and its salt, sodium methanoate, HCOONa.

Alternatively, we could use a weak base (to neutralise added acid) together with its conjugate acid (to neutralise added base). Thus a solution of

ammonia, NH_3 ($pK_a = 9.2$), and ammonium chloride, NH_4Cl, will buffer pH at around 9.

We will now look at the following example: making a weak acid buffer solution of about 5.

Examination of *table 5.3* (page 80) shows that propanoic acid has a pK_a of 4.9. This is a good start. It suggests that a mixture of propanoic acid and sodium propanoate would work well.

Now let's examine the pH values of mixtures of different concentrations, starting with $600 \, cm^3$ of $1 \, mol \, dm^{-3}$ propanoic acid and $400 \, cm^3$ $2 \, mol \, dm^{-3}$ sodium propanoate solution.

The equilibrium constant K_a for propanoic acid is $1.3 \times 10^{-5} \, mol \, dm^{-3}$. The equation linking this to the concentration of protons (what we need for pH calculation) is

$$K_a = \frac{[C_2H_5COO^-(aq)][H^+(aq)]}{[C_2H_5COOH(aq)]}$$

so that

$$[H^+(aq)] = K_a \times \frac{[C_2H_5COOH(aq)]}{[C_2H_5COO^-(aq)]}$$

The concentration of acid and base, the amount of each in the total mixture, must be calculated and substituted.

$$\text{concentration} = \text{number of moles/volume}$$

$$\text{total volume} = 600 + 400 = 1000 \, dm^3$$

$$[C_2H_5COOH(aq)] = \frac{(600 \, cm^3 \times 1 \, mol \, dm^{-3})}{(600 \, cm^3 + 400 \, cm^3)}$$

$$= 0.6 \, mol \, dm^{-3}$$

$$[C_2H_5COO^-(aq)] = \frac{(400 \, cm^3 \times 2 \, mol \, dm^{-3})}{(600 \, cm^3 + 400 \, cm^3)}$$

$$= 0.8 \, mol \, dm^{-3}$$

Now the pH can be found:

$$[H^+(aq)] = K_a \frac{[C_2H_5COOH]}{[C_2H_5COO^-]}$$

$$= \frac{1.3 \times 10^{-5} \, mol \, dm^{-3} \times 0.6 \, mol \, dm^{-3}}{0.8 \, mol \, dm^{-3}}$$

$$= 9.75 \times 10^{-6} \, mol \, dm^{-3}$$

so

$$pH = -\log_{10}(9.75 \times 10^{-6})$$

so

$$pH = -(-5.01) = 5.01$$

The mathematics of this type of problem can be demanding to begin with. You need practice! Do the calculations below using the data from *table 5.3* (page 80).

SAQ 5.17

Calculate the pH of a solution consisting of:

a 500 cm^3 of 0.1 mol dm^{-3} methanoic acid and 500 cm^3 of 0.2 mol dm^{-3} sodium methanoate;

b 200 cm^3 of 0.5 mol dm^{-3} benzoic acid and 800 cm^3 of 0.5 mol dm^{-3} sodium benzoate.

Of course, there is a limit to the efficiency of buffers, as we have indicated above. Rain-water has a pH of 5.7 in unpolluted regions, because it dissolves carbon dioxide, which in solution forms the weak acid carbonic acid, H_2CO_3(aq), with a pK_a of 6.4. This buffer solution will accommodate small additions of acid and alkali. But in highly polluted industrial regions, or in rural areas that lie down-wind of such contamination, the pH of rain-water is around 4, and in extreme cases may even be less than 2, so-called 'acid rain'. Here the atmospheric pollutant gases are sulphur dioxide and sulphur trioxide, arising from the combustion of fossil fuels containing sulphur, and nitrogen monoxide and nitrogen dioxide, due mainly to nitrogen oxidation in internal combustion engines. They dissolve in rain-water and overwhelm the buffering effect.

Buffers in the bathroom and beyond

Tucked away on bathroom shelves and cabinets are all sorts of products whose acidity or alkalinity has to be controlled. From antacids and eye-drops to skin creams and baby lotion, buffers are used to maintain an appropriate pH. Safety is most important – the pH control system must be harmless. Non-toxic buffers have to be used.

Baby lotion is buffered – 'pH balanced' as the adverts claim – to minimise nappy rash (*figure 5.11*). This skin irritation is caused by ammonia.

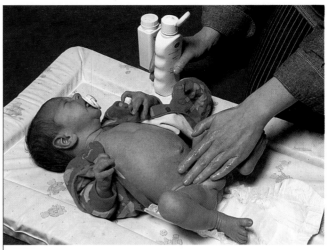

● **Figure 5.11** Buffers benefit babies!

Dirty nappies contain just the right ingredients for making ammonia – urine and faeces. The latter contains a bacterium, *Bacillus ammoniagenes*, which lives in the baby's colon. Urine contains water and urea. An enzyme from the bacterium reacts with water and urea, forming ammonia in reactions summarised by this equation:

$$CO(NH_2)_2(aq) + H_2O(l) \longrightarrow 2NH_3(aq) + CO_2(aq)$$

urea   ammonia

These bacteria multiply well in the pH range 7–9, but not at all at pH6. Consequently, baby lotion is buffered to keep the pH about 6 – around the pH of the skin itself. The offending bacteria do not multiply and ammonia production is limited. Nappies should be washed well to kill these bacteria. A hot water wash at 60°C does this.

Washing powders include buffers. Without them their high alkalinity would damage skin – they would not be kind to your hands! Buffers are also used in washing powders containing enzymes, to let them operate at the optimum conditions. For example, protease, an enzyme that breaks down proteins, operates best at pH from 9 to 10. Interestingly, this enzyme is produced by the bacterium *Bacillus licheniformis*, which would itself be digested by protease at this pH. The biotechnologists who produce this enzyme keep their fermenters at pH7 to stop this. Guess how!

Drugs must be manufactured with an eye to pH control. Most drugs are a mixture of substances, and some ingredients could affect the optimum pH without the use of buffers.

SAQ 5.18

Intravenous drugs are carefully buffered. What pH should be aimed for, and what might happen if pH was not controlled?

SAQ 5.19

Calculate the pH of the following buffer solutions:

a 500 cm³ of 0.1 mol dm⁻³ benzoic acid and 500 cm³ of 0.1 mol dm⁻³ sodium benzoate solution.

b 20 cm³ of 0.1 mol dm⁻³ ethanoic acid and 80 cm³ of 0.2 mol dm⁻³ potassium ethanoate solution.

c 100 cm³ of 0.1 mol dm⁻³ ammonium hydroxide solution and 100 cm³ of 0.2 mol dm⁻³ ammonium chloride solution.

d Methylamine (CH_3NH_2) has a $pK_b = 3.36$. Calculate its pK_a, its K_a, and the pH of 20 cm³ of a 0.001 mol dm⁻³ solution of methylamine and 10 cm³ of 0.005 mol dm⁻³ methylammonium chloride ($CH_3NH_3^+Cl^-$).

SAQ 5.20

Citric acid has a pK_a of 3.1 and boric acid has a pK_a of 9.2. Which of these would be best to use in making a buffer for eye-drops? Suggest an appropriate mixture of ingredients to buffer the eye-drops at around 7.5.

Introducing K_{sp}, the solubility product

Sea life and solubility

Figure 5.12 shows two forms of marine life. Both of them grow in sea-water, using compounds dissolved in it. Coral is made largely of calcium carbonate, and diatoms consist of silica. (Diatoms are a kind of algae with flinty shells.) These are the same chemicals that go to make the white cliffs of Dover and the sands of Great Yarmouth beach, respectively.

Coral and diatoms extract their minerals from sea-water – minerals we think of as being insoluble. They *are* insoluble in sea-water, but in pure

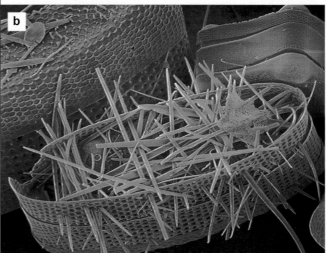

● *Figure 5.12*

a Corals are animals that produce deposits of calcium carbonate, $CaCO_3$. These deposits often build up into large and beautiful structures.

b Diatoms have shells made of silica, SiO_3. The magnification in this photograph is ×600.

water or the slightly acidic water of unpolluted rain this is not the case. They are slightly soluble. Indeed, any salt, oxide or carbonate – any mineral in fact – dissolves in water to some extent. Some, like sodium chloride, are very soluble indeed – a kilogram of common salt needs less than 3 cubic decimetres of cold water to dissolve it and form a saturated solution. In contrast, a kilogram of calcium carbonate requires about 77 000 cubic decimetres of cold water, i.e. 77 tonnes of it. This sounds a lot until you consider this is only a small swimming pool full of water, one which is 10 m long, 5 m wide and just over 1.5 m deep.

The definition of K_{sp}

When a solid like calcium carbonate is stirred up in 100 g of pure water at 298 K, it eventually forms a saturated solution in which 1.3×10^{-5} moles of calcium carbonate (1.3×10^{-3} g) dissolves. It only dissolves because a small proportion of the ions in the solid go into solution. An equilibrium is set up as follows, (where 'aq' means lots of water):

$$CaCO_3(s) \overset{aq}{\rightleftharpoons} Ca^{2+}(aq) + CO_3{}^{2-}(aq)$$

Very little of the calcium carbonate actually dissolves, so the equilibrium is well to the left. The equilibrium constant is therefore very small:

$$K_c = \frac{[Ca^{2+}(aq)][CO_3{}^{2-}(aq)]}{[CaCO_3(s)]}$$

This is not a homogeneous equilibrium, i.e. one in which all the ions are in the same state, e.g. as ions in solution or gases in an atmosphere. This is a **heterogeneous equilibrium**. The bits making it up are in different states, in solution and as a solid. In this case the concentration of calcium carbonate remains unchanged because it is a solid, so this value too is a constant. Thus K_c, which is a constant, is equal to $[Ca^{2+}(aq)][CO_3{}^{2-}(aq)]$ divided by another constant. We can therefore say that the *product* of the ions in solution, $[Ca^{2+}(aq)][CO_3{}^{2-}(aq)]$, is also constant. Because this ion product indicates the solubility of the calcium carbonate, we call it the **solubility product**, K_{sp}:

$$K_{sp} = [Ca^{2+}(aq)][CO_3{}^{2-}(aq)] = K_c[CaCO_3(s)]$$

In general terms, if the ionic compound A_xB_y is only very slightly soluble in water then

$$K_{sp} = [A]^x[B]^y$$

For example, calcium phosphate establishes the following equilibrium in water:

$$Ca_3(PO_4)_2(s) \rightleftharpoons 3Ca^{2+}(aq) + 2PO_4{}^{3-}(aq)$$

If we think of this in terms of the general ionic compound A_xB_y, with $A = Ca$, $x = 3$ and $B = PO_4$, $y = 2$, we can easily see that for this equilibrium

$$K_{sp} = [Ca^{2+}]^3 [PO_4{}^{3-}]^2$$

SAQ 5.21

Write the formula for the solubility product for the following sparingly soluble salts in terms of ion concentration:

a   silver chloride, $AgCl(s)$, $K_{sp} = 2.0 \times 10^{-10} mol^2 dm^{-6}$;

b   silver sulphide, $Ag_2S(s)$, $K_{sp} = 6.3 \times 10^{-50} mol^3 dm^{-9}$;

c   zinc cyanide, $Zn(CN)_2(s)$, $K_{sp} = 2.6 \times 10^{-13} mol^3 dm^{-9}$.

Which of the three salts is least soluble in water, and which the most?

Making predictions with K_{sp}

We know that for calcium carbonate

$$K_{sp} = [Ca^{2+}(aq)][CO_3{}^{2-}(aq)]$$
$$= 5.0 \times 10^{-9} mol^2 dm^{-6}$$

If the product of the concentrations of calcium ions and carbonate ions in a solution can be made bigger than K_{sp}, then solid calcium carbonate must begin to form. We say it is 'precipitated' as a solid. This is exactly what happens inside shellfish. The living organism concentrates the ions so that solid calcium carbonate precipitates, just where it wants it to build its shell.

If the product of the concentration of calcium ions and carbonate ions is less than K_{sp}, then no precipitated solid appears. Indeed the reverse would happen. Any calcium carbonate in the water would dissolve. This happens deep in our oceans. The solubility product of calcium carbonate increases with increased pressure and lower temperature. Any shells sinking into the depths will start to dissolve.

A third possibility exists – that the product of the concentrations of calcium and carbonate ions equals K_{sp}. This indicates that we have a solution where:

■ no precipitation will occur if there is no change;

■ no more calcium carbonate can dissolve.

This is the situation for a saturated solution.

Some calculations

The solubility of silver bromide, AgBr, in water is $7.19 \times 10^{-7} mol\, dm^{-3}$ at 25 °C. Calculate the solubility product of silver bromide at this temperature.

First we write the equilibrium:

$$AgBr(s) \rightleftharpoons Ag^+(aq) + Br^-(aq)$$

The equation shows that for every mole of silver bromide that dissolves, a mole each of silver ions and bromide ions go into solution. In a saturated solution (one in which no more silver bromide can be dissolved) we know how much silver bromide is present in a decimetre cube of water. It is 7.19×10^{-7} mol. Therefore the concentration of each ion in solution is 7.19×10^{-7} mol dm^{-3}. We substitute these values in the expression for the solubility product:

$$
\begin{aligned}
K_{sp} &= [Ag^+] \times [Br^-] \\
&= (7.19 \times 10^{-7} \, mol \, dm^{-3}) \\
&\quad \times (7.19 \times 10^{-7} \, mol \, dm^{-3}) \\
&= 7.19 \times 7.19 \times 10^{-14} \, mol^2 \, dm^{-6} \\
&= 51.7 \times 10^{-14} \, mol^2 \, dm^{-6} \\
&= 5.17 \times 10^{-13} \, mol^2 \, dm^{-6}
\end{aligned}
$$

Things are not always quite so simple. Follow how we calculate K_{sp} for calcium fluoride, CaF_2. The solubility at 298 K is 1.8×10^{-3} g per 100 g of water, and the relative atomic masses for calcium and fluorine are 40 and 19 respectively.

Since the solubility product needs the concentration to be in mol dm^{-3}, the first step is to calculate solubility in these terms.

1 mol of calcium fluoride has a mass of $40 + (2 \times 19) = 78$ g

1.8×10^{-3} g calcium fluoride dissolve in 100 g water

so $\dfrac{1.8 \times 10^{-3}}{78}$ mol calcium fluoride dissolve in 100 g water

i.e. 2.3×10^{-5} mol calcium fluoride dissolve in 100 g water

so 2.3×10^{-4} mol calcium fluoride dissolve in 1000 g water

This is very close to being a solution with a concentration of 2.3×10^{-4} mol calcium fluoride per 1 dm^{-3} solution. First, we assume that 1000 g of water at 298 K has a volume of 1 dm^3, which it almost has. Secondly, we assume that 1 dm^3 of water containing 2.3×10^{-4} mol dissolved calcium fluoride is equivalent to 1 dm^3 of the actual

solution. It very nearly is, because the solubility is so minimal – not an assumption you can make about a soluble salt like sodium chloride.

The equilibrium is

$$CaF_2(s) \rightleftharpoons Ca^{2+}(aq) + 2F^-(aq)$$

so

$$K_{sp} = [Ca^{2+}][F^-]^2 \, mol^3 \, dm^{-9}$$

i.e.

$$
\begin{aligned}
K_{sp} &= (2.3 \times 10^{-4}) \times (4.6 \times 10^{-4})^2 \, mol^3 \, dm^{-9} \\
&= 48.7 \times 10^{-12} \, mol^3 \, dm^{-9} \\
&= 4.87 \times 10^{-11} \, mol^3 \, dm^{-9}
\end{aligned}
$$

SAQ 5.22

a Why are the units for K_{sp} for calcium fluoride different from those for K_{sp} for silver bromide?

b Why is the concentration of fluoride ions double that of calcium ions?

c Why is the concentration of fluoride ions squared in K_{sp} for calcium fluoride?

d What would be the units for the solubility product of calcium phosphate $Ca_3(PO_4)_2(s)$?

Similar calculations can be done to work out solubilities from solubility products. Consider the case of calcium carbonate. The solubility product of this compound is 5.0×10^{-9} mol^2 dm^{-6}.

Let x be the solubility of calcium carbonate in water. In a saturated solution we have the following equilibrium:

$$CaCO_3(s) \rightleftharpoons Ca^{2+}(aq) + CO_3^{2-}(aq)$$

so

$$
\begin{aligned}
K_{sp} &= [Ca^{2+}][CO_3^{2-}] \\
&= (x) \times (x)
\end{aligned}
$$

i.e.

$$x^2 = 5.0 \times 10^{-9} \, mol^2 \, dm^{-6}$$

so

$$x = 7.1 \times 10^{-5} \, mol \, dm^{-3}$$

Therefore the solubility of calcium carbonate is 7.1×10^{-5} mol dm^{-3} under the conditions at which the solubility product was measured.

Precipitation: will it or won't it?

The photograph in *figure 5.13* shows a solution of potassium iodide being poured into a solution of lead nitrate. An intense yellow precipitate of lead iodide is formed. The question is, would this always happen no matter what the concentration of the solutions was?

We will consider an example, in which $60\,cm^3$ of $0.002\,mol\,dm^{-3}$ potassium iodide is mixed with $40\,cm^3$ of $0.001\,mol\,dm^{-3}$ lead nitrate solution. The solubility product of lead iodide in aqueous solution is $7.1 \times 10^{-9}\,mol^3\,dm^{-9}$. Will there be a precipitate of lead iodide?

We need to find the concentration of lead and iodide ions in $mol\,dm^{-3}$. The total volume of the mixture is $(60 + 40)\,cm^3 = 0.1\,dm^3$. The amount of iodide ions present in solution is

$(0.002)\,mol\,dm^{-3} \times (60 \times 10^{-3})\,dm^3$
   (note conversion of cm^3 to dm^3)
$= 1.2 \times 10^{-4}\,mol$ in $0.1\,dm^3$
   (check the units make sense)

So the concentration of iodide ions is 1.2×10^{-3}.

A similar calculation shows the amount of lead ions in the solution to be $4.0 \times 10^{-5}\,mol$. Check this is the case for yourself.
Therefore

$$[I^-(aq)] = 1.2 \times 10^{-3}\,mol\,dm^{-3}$$

and

$$[Pb^{2+}(aq)] = 4.0 \times 10^{-4}\,mol\,dm^{-3}$$

● **Figure 5.13** Potassium iodide and lead nitrate react to form a yellow precipitate of lead iodide, leaving potassium ions and nitrate ions in solution.

so the 'ion product'

$[Pb^{2+}(aq)]\,[I^-(aq)]^2 = 4.0 \times 10^{-4}$
$\qquad \times (1.2 \times 10^{-3})^2\,mol^3\,dm^{-9}$
$\qquad = 5.8 \times 10^{-10}\,mol^3\,dm^{-9}$

This value is less than the solubility product for lead iodide at $298\,K$, so there will not be a precipitate when the solutions are mixed.

SAQ 5.23

Suppose the concentration of each solution was increased by a factor of three. Would a precipitate of lead iodide form now?

Using solubility products: the common-ion effect

A statement of the common-ion effect is: the solubility of any ionic compound is less in a solution containing a common ion than in pure water. For example, silver chloride, $AgCl(s)$, has a very low solubility in water. Its solubility product is 2.0×10^{-10} at $298\,K$. What would happen of we could inject some more chloride ions into a saturated solution of silver chloride?

We can start with the mathematics of K_{sp}. Writing the equation the other way round we have

$$[Ag^+(aq)][Cl^-(aq)] = K_{sp}$$

i.e. the two concentrations multiplied together have a constant value. Now try to make three reasoned predictions:

■ What should happen to the concentration of silver ions in the saturated solution if the concentration of chloride ions was increased?
■ In practical terms, how can this change go ahead?
■ What should you *see* if chloride ions were added to a saturated solution of silver chloride?

This can be done. The extra chloride ions could come from the addition of potassium chloride solution. The result of such an addition can be seen in *figure 5.14*. Were your predictions any good?

SAQ 5.24

Name another salt (not a chloride) that you could add to a saturated solution of silver chloride to cause some of it to precipitate.

● *Figure 5.14* Potassium chloride solution is added to saturated silver chloride solution. A precipitate of silver chloride forms. The chloride ion, common to both solutions, is responsible. As the concentration of chloride ions increases in the flask, the concentration of silver ions must fall to compensate, to keep the solubility product constant. The only way for this to happen is for some of the silver ions to come out of solution. They do so as part of a silver chloride precipitate.

SAQ 5.25

Lime water is saturated calcium hydroxide solution, $Ca(OH)_2(aq)$. Suppose you were to add a pellet of sodium hydroxide to this and shake it up.

a What ions would the calcium hydroxide contribute to the mixture?

b What ions would the sodium hydroxide contribute to the mixture?

c Which of these ions is common to both?

d What effect would this common ion have on the concentration of the calcium ions in the solution?

e What would you see as a result?

SAQ 5.26

Although there is no solubility product quoted for sodium chloride, it is possible to precipitate this salt from a saturated solution using the common ion effect. Suggest ways of doing this, and plan an investigation to test your ideas. **Warning:** Check your suggestions with your teacher before you experiment – your ideas may well be inherently dangerous!

SAQ 5.27

The solubility product of barium carbonate in pure water at 298K is $5.5 \times 10^{-10}\,\text{mol}^2\text{dm}^{-6}$. Would you expect the solubility of barium carbonate to be different in hard tap-water and in sea-water, and, if so, how and why?

Looking back and looking forwards

We opened this book by looking at the Earth – a great reaction vessel in which millions of chemical reactions are fuelled (in the long run) by solar energy. You should now be in a better position to understand some of these reactions, and in particular to think about questions of quantity.

You may in future become a professional scientist – perhaps a biologist researching the effect of low-level ozone on crop development, or a geologist investigating what our climate was like in the past. Perhaps you will use your science as an anaesthetist or as a preserver of ancient artifacts in a museum. If so, you will probably ask questions about chemical reactions: 'To what extent is parchment damage due to acidic gases in the atmosphere?' (*how far*), and 'How long did it take for atmospheric carbon dioxide to be fixed in limestone deposits?' (*how fast*). Questions like these could become part of your professional life.

You may, of course, never study chemistry again. However, you will become (we hope) a tax-paying member of society with the right to vote and a voice in our future. You may well be in a position some day to put a chemist on the spot. Whether you are debating the choice of catalytic converter for your new car or considering the use of biodegradable packaging, the questions that chemists ask, 'How far?', and 'How fast?', should come to mind. With any luck you'll understand the answers – or whether the respondent is trying to pull a fast one!

SUMMARY

■ Chemicals may be described as acids and bases. There are several definitions of acids and bases, of which the Brønsted–Lowry definition is perhaps the most useful: an acid is a proton donor and a base is a proton acceptor.

■ The strength of an acid depends on its ability to lose a proton. A strong acid will ionise almost completely in solution.

■ The acid dissociation constant, K_a, is a measure of the strength of an acid. A more convenient scale for the comparison of acid strengths is provided by pK_a, where

$$pK_a = -\log_{10}[K_a]$$

■ The strength of a base depends on its ability to gain a proton.

■ K_w is the ionic product of water:

$$K_w = [H^+][OH^-] = 1.00 \times 10^{-14}\,mol^2\,dm^{-6}$$

■ The pH is a measure of the concentration of protons in a solution:

$$pH = -\log_{10}[H^+]$$

■ Indicators are chemicals that change colour over particular ranges of pH values. When an acid is added to a base, there will be a particular point in the reaction where the quantity of acid is exactly sufficient to neutralise the base. This point is called the *end-point*, at which the reaction has proceeded exactly to completion and no further. Indicators may be used to show when an end-point has been reached.

■ A buffer solution is a mixture of an acid and its conjugate base. It will maintain a reasonably constant pH value when moderate amounts of acid or base are added to it. Buffer solutions are especially important in biological solutions and industrial processes.

■ The solubility product, K_{sp}, is a measure of the solubility of a solid. If the ionic compound A_xB_y is only slightly soluble in water, then

$$K_{sp} = [A]^x[B]^y$$

■ The common-ion effect is that the solubility of any ionic compound is less in a solution containing a common ion than in pure water.

Questions

1 The data on the right were calculated using a spreadsheet. They show how incremental changes in the concentration of a Brønsted–Lowry acid affect the pH of a mixture with its conjugate base. The concentration of the conjugate base is held constant at $1\,mol\,dm^{-3}$. The volumes of both acid and base are each $1\,dm^{-3}$. What can you infer from the data?

pK_a of the acid (propanoic acid) = 4.9

What would you predict if the concentration of the acid was held constant and the concentration of the conjugate base was varied? Test this prediction using a spreadsheet, or by mathematical argument.

2 The table below shows some experimental data from an investigation of the solubility product of silver chloride at $298\,K$. Copy the table and calculate the missing data, and suggest a pair of values for the concentrations of each ion that would give a saturated solution of silver chloride.

Concentration of Brønsted–Lowry acid/$mol\,dm^{-3}$	pH
0.1	5.90
0.2	5.60
0.3	5.42
0.4	5.30
0.5	5.20
0.6	5.12
0.7	5.05
0.8	5.00
0.9	4.95
1.0	4.90
1.1	4.86
1.2	4.82
1.3	4.79
1.4	4.75
1.5	4.72
1.6	4.70
1.7	4.67
1.8	4.64
1.9	4.62
2.0	4.60

$[Ag^+(aq)]$	$[Cl^-(aq)]$	K_{sp}
1.34×10^{-5}	1.34×10^{-5}	1.80×10^{-10}
1.32×10^{-5}		1.80×10^{-10}
1.25×10^{-5}		
	1.30×10^{-5}	

Answers to self-assessment questions

Chapter 1

1.1 When one mole of sulphuric acid is neutralised by two moles of sodium hydroxide, two moles of water molecules are formed:

$$H_2SO_4(aq) + 2NaOH(aq)$$
$$\longrightarrow Na_2SO_4(aq) + 2H_2O(l)$$

For every mole of water molecules formed, 57.14 kJ of heat energy are evolved, so in this case (2×57.14) kJ = 114.28 kJ of heat energy are produced.

1.2 *Figure 1.18* represents atomisation:
$$\tfrac{1}{2}O_2(g) \longrightarrow O(g)$$

Figure 1.19 represents neutralisation:
$$H^+(aq) + OH^-(aq) \longrightarrow H_2O(l)$$

Figure 1.20 may represent formation:
$$H_2(g) + 2C(s) \longrightarrow C_2H_2(g)$$

or combustion:
$$C(s) + O_2(g) \longrightarrow CO_2(g)$$

Figure 1.21 represents solution:
$$NaCl(s) \overset{H_2O}{\longrightarrow} Na^+(aq) + Cl^-(aq)$$

Figure 1.22 represents hydration:
$$Na^+(g) \overset{H_2O}{\longrightarrow} Na^+(aq)$$

1.3 Bond **d** > (is stronger than) **b** > **a** > **c**.

Chapter 2

2.1 Lead oxide is reduced to lead. Carbon monoxide is the reducing agent.

Carbon monoxide is oxidised to carbon dioxide. Lead oxide is the oxidising agent.

2.2 When iron reacts with chlorine, iron metal is oxidised to iron(III) ions, Fe^{3+}. Chlorine is the oxidising agent, and is itself reduced to chloride ions, Cl^-.

2.3 **a** Copper atoms are oxidised and lose two electrons each to become copper ions, Cu^{2+}. Iodine atoms within the molecule are reduced, and each gains an electron to become a negative ion, I^-.

b Each iron(III) ion, Fe^{3+}, gains an electron and is reduced to an iron(II) ion, Fe^{2+}.

c Iron is oxidised to iron(II), and copper(II) is reduced to copper as two electrons per atom are lost by iron atoms and gained by copper ions.

d If we assume magnesium and oxide ions are formed, then magnesium atoms are oxidised to magnesium(II) ions by losing two electrons per atom. These electrons are gained by oxygen atoms, which are reduced to form ions with a charge of -2.

e Copper(II) ions, Cu^{2+}, are reduced to copper(I) ions, Cu^+, by gaining electrons from silver atoms. The silver atoms are oxidised.

2.4 A uranium atom, like all atoms, has an oxidation number of zero.

2.5 The oxidation number of the oxide ion, O^{2-}, is -2.

The oxidation number of the hydrogen ion, H^+, is $+1$.

2.6 $+2$

2.7 -1

2.8 $+4$

2.9 In ClF, the oxidation number of chlorine = $+1$.

In CaF_2, the oxidation number of calcium = $+2$.

In XeF_4, the oxidation number of xenon = $+4$.

2.10 Lead(IV) is reduced to lead(II) by electrons.

2.11 Magnesium metal, which is highly reactive, would lose atoms into solution as positive ions, leaving an excess of electrons in the metal. Magnesium would therefore be negative with respect to the electrolyte. Silver metal would be the opposite. If both half-cells were brought together as a cell, electrons would flow from the magnesium towards the positive terminal – the silver. The magnesium atoms, which would lose electrons to become ions in the electrolyte, would be oxidised; the silver cations would be reduced to atoms.

2.12 Half reactions:
$$Ni(s) \longrightarrow Ni^{2+}(aq) + 2e^-$$
$$Co^{3+}(aq) + e^- \longrightarrow Co^{2+}(aq)$$

Full reaction:
$$Ni(s) + 2Co^{3+}(aq) \longrightarrow Ni^{2+}(aq) + 2Co^{2+}(aq)$$

Cell statement:
$$Ni(s) \mid Ni^{2+}(aq) \mathbin{\|} Co^{3+}(aq) \mid Co^{2+}(aq)$$

Therefore
$$E^{\ominus}(298)_{cell} = E^{\ominus}(298)_{right} - E^{\ominus}(298)_{left}$$
$$= +1.82\,V - (-0.25)\,V$$
$$= +2.07\,V$$

The positive answer indicates that the reaction will proceed: Ni will reduce Co^{3+} ions to Co^{2+} ions.

2.13 $MnO_4^- + 4H^+ + 3Cr^{2+}$
$\longrightarrow MnO_2 + 2H_2O + 3Cr^{3+}$

2.14 Each dilution of $Ag^+(aq)$ by a factor of 10 produces a drop of 0.06 V. By extrapolation, dilution to $0.0001\,mol\,dm^{-3}$ causes the electrode potential to fall to 0.56 V.

Chapter 3

3.1 $Cu(s) \mid Cu^{2+}(aq) \mathbin{\|} Fe^{2+}(aq) \mid Fe(s)$

Theoretically the standard cell potential should be positive for the cell to produce electrons, which will result in copper ions being reduced to copper. This is the case as shown below:
$$E^{\ominus}(298)_{cell} = E^{\ominus}(298)_{right} - E^{\ominus}(298)_{left}$$
$$= (+0.34\,V) - (-0.44\,V)$$
$$= +0.77\,V$$

3.2 For every copper ion reduced to a copper atom, an atom of iron is oxidised to become an ion, Fe^{2+}. Thus the rate of change of concentration of copper ions = the rate of change of concentration of iron atoms = $-0.0025\,mol\,dm^{-3}\,s^{-1}$.

3.3 Experimental evidence shows that the rate of reaction is directly proportional to the concentration of cyclopropane. If the concentration if cyclopropane is halved, the rate of reaction is halved.

3.4 The reaction is first order with respect to cyclopropane and first order overall.

3.5 Yes. Figures 3.7 and 3.8 give an approximate half-life of 17.5 min.

3.6 By titrating small samples of the reaction mixture with standardised base, for example $1.0\,mol\,dm^{-3}$ aqueous sodium hydroxide, you could find the concentration of hydrochloric acid as the reaction progressed. You could also monitor this concentration using either a pH meter or a conductivity meter. Both devices respond to changes in hydrogen ion concentration, which is itself an indication of the concentration of hydrochloric acid.

3.7 The reaction rate = $k[N_2O_5]$, so the order of the reaction is 1.

3.8

3.9 $2C_2H_2(g) + 5O_2(g) \longrightarrow 4CO_2(g) + 2H_2O(g)$

3.10 The concentration is higher in *figure 3.22a*. The rate of reaction will therefore be greater in *figure 3.22a*.

3.11 A spark or match might provide the activation energy.

3.12 *Figure 3.29a* has lower entropy than *figure 3.29b*, so *figure 3.29b* represents the more stable situation.

Chapter 4

4.1 The ten moles of hydrogen iodide begin to dissociate, forming hydrogen and iodine:

$$2HI(g) \rightleftharpoons H_2(g) + I_2(g)$$

For every molecule of iodine formed, two molecules of hydrogen iodide have to split up. To form 0.68 moles of iodine molecules, 2×0.68 moles of hydrogen iodide must dissociate. This means a total loss of 1.36 moles of hydrogen iodide, from 10 down to 8.64 moles.

4.2 Low values of K_c tell you that an equilibrium mixture consists mostly of reactants and there is very little product – the equilibrium is to the left. The mathematics of K_c should make this clear:

In the equilibrium $\quad A + B \rightleftharpoons C + D$

$$K_c = \frac{[C][D]}{[A][B]}$$

If K_c is small, [C][D] is much less than [A][B]. If K_c was $0.001 = 1/1000$, then [C][D] (the concentration of C times the concentration of D) would be 1000 times smaller than [A][B].

4.3

a $K_c = \dfrac{[N_2O_4(g)]}{[NO_2(g)]^2}$ $\mathrm{mol^{-1}\,dm^3}$

b $K_c = \dfrac{[NO^2(g)]^2}{[NO(g)]^2[O_2(g)]}$ $\mathrm{mol^{-1}\,dm^3}$

c $K_c = \dfrac{[NO(g)]^4\,[H_2O(g)]^6}{[NH_3(g)]^4\,[O_2(g)]^5}$ $\mathrm{mol\,dm^{-3}}$

4.4 If the concentration of iodine $[I_2(g)]$ is increased, then to keep the value of K_c the same, the concentration of hydrogen iodide $[HI(g)]$ must also increase. For this to happen the equilibrium shifts to the right, so minimising the effect of the initial change.

4.5

a If the temperature of an exothermic equilibrium is increased, the system of reactants and products gains heat. Le Chatelier's principle indicates that the system will respond to minimise this heat gain, so less product will be formed and hence less heat energy will be given out. The equilibrium will shift to the left, and the value of K_c will be reduced.

b If the temperature of an endothermic reaction is increased, there is an overall increase in heat energy of the system. Le Chatelier's principle indicates that the system will respond to minimise this heat gain by producing more product (a change which requires an input of heat). The equilibrium will shift to the right and the value of K_c will be increased.

c If the temperature of an endothermic equilibrium is decreased, there is a net loss of energy from the system. To counter this, less product is formed so that less heat energy is required. The equilibrium shifts to the left and the value of K_c falls.

4.6 The remaining gas mixture consists of unreacted gases from the air (mainly nitrogen with a small percentage of argon).

If all the oxygen in the furnace were used up during combustion, the final mixture would contain about 20% sulphur dioxide by volume. This would hamper the second stage of the process – more oxygen would have to be supplied.

4.7

a Le Chatelier's principle predicts that the equilibrium shifts to counteract any change in the conditions. If sulphur trioxide is removed, the equilibrium shifts to counter this, so more sulphur trioxide is produced.

b The reaction is exothermic. If the temperature is lowered there will be a reduction in heat energy in the system. The equilibrium will shift to compensate for this, so that more sulphur trioxide and more heat energy are produced.

c Increased pressure pushes the molecules of gas together, increasing their concentration. This change is countered by the equilibrium shifting so that more sulphur dioxide and oxygen molecules react to form sulphur trioxide, in each case producing one molecule from two and lowering the concentration. Hence to produce more sulphur trioxide, the pressure should be high.

In practice the pressure is seldom increased. More expensive plant would be required, and there would be an increased risk of sulphur oxides escaping to pollute the atmosphere.

4.8
a $K_p = \dfrac{\{p(NO)\}^2}{\{p(N_2)\}\,\{p(O_2)\}}$ no units

b $K_p = \dfrac{\{p(C_2H_5OH)\}}{\{p(C_2H_4)\}\,\{p(H_2O)\}}$ Pa^{-1}

Chapter 5

5.1 In the equilibrium, the water molecule gains a proton to form $H_3O^+(aq)$, so H_2O is a Brønsted–Lowry base. Its conjugate acid is the H_3O^+ species, which with its extra proton is richer in protons than a water molecule.

5.2 The conjugate pairs are NH_3 (base) with NH_4^+ (acid), and H_2O (acid) with OH^- (base). In both cases the conjugate acids are richer in protons than their conjugate bases.

5.3 In these examples, the conjugate acids and bases are linked by a line.

a $H_2SO_4(l) \xrightarrow{H_2O} 2H^+(aq) + SO_4^{2-}(aq)$
B–L acid B–L base

b $C_6H_5COOH(aq) \xrightarrow{H_2O} C_6H_5COO^-(aq) + H^+(aq)$
B-L acid B-L base

c
$CH_3NH_2(aq) + H_2O(l) \longrightarrow CH_3NH_3^+(aq) + OH^-(aq)$
B–L base   B–L acid   B–L acid   B–L base

d $NH_3(g) + HCl(g) \longrightarrow NH_4^+(s) + Cl^-(s)$
B–L base   B–L acid   B–L acid   B–L base

5.4 Pure water is a poor conductor of electricity, which shows that it carries very few ions that can carry a direct current.

5.5 $K_c = \dfrac{[H^+][OH^-]}{[H_2O]}$

K_c is very small, so the concentrations of the products must be very much smaller then the concentration of water itself. This indicates that only a tiny proportion of pure water exists at any one time as protons and hydroxide ions, a deduction backed by the evidence that water is a poor conductor of electricity.

5.6 **a** 3.52

b 2.00

c 7.40

5.7 **a** 0.0

b 0.3

c 1.4

d The aqueous solution contains 3 g of hydrogen chloride, HCl, per dm^3. To find the pH we need the hydrogen ion concentration in $mol\,dm^{-3}$.

The relative molecular mass of HCl
$= (1 + 35.5) = 36.5$.

Thus the concentration of hydrogen chloride
$$= 3/36.5\,mol\,dm^{-3}$$
$$= 0.082\,mol\,dm^{-3}$$

Because the hydrogen chloride dissociates completely to form hydrogen ions and chlorine ions, the concentration of hydrogen ions is $0.082\,mol\,dm^{-3}$. The pH of this acid
$= -\log_{10}[H^+] = -\log_{10}[0.082] = 1.1$.

e Potassium hydroxide dissociates completely in solution:

$$KOH(s) \xrightarrow{H_2O} K^+(aq) + OH^-(aq)$$
$$\text{0.001 mol} \qquad \text{0.001 mol} \qquad \text{0.001 mol}$$

The concentration of hydroxide ions is the same as the concentration of the potassium hydroxide.

Method 1:

$$K_w = [H^+][OH^-] = 1 \times 10^{-14} mol^2 dm^{-6}$$

so

$$[H^+] = 1 \times 10^{-14} mol^2 dm^{-6}/[OH^-]$$
$$= 1 \times 10^{-14} mol^2 dm^{-6}/0.001\,mol\,dm^{-3}$$
$$= 1 \times 10^{-11} mol\,dm^{-3}$$

The pH of this acid

$$= -\log_{10}[H^+] = -\log_{10}[10^{-11}] = 11.0$$

Method 2: $\quad [OH^-] = 0.001\,mol\,dm^{-3}$

Now $pOH = -\log_{10}[OH^-] = -\log_{10}[0.001] = 3.0$

So $pH = 14.0 - pOH = 14.0 - 3.0 = 11.0$

f Sodium hydroxide ionises completely in aqueous solution:

$$NaOH(s) \xrightarrow{H_2O} Na^+(aq) + OH^-(aq)$$

The relative molecular mass of NaOH = (23 + 16 + 1) = 40.

An aqueous solution containing 0.2 g of NaOH per dm^3 contains (0.2/40) mol NaOH, i.e. $5 \times 10^{-3} mol\,dm^{-3}$. The concentration of hydroxide ions is therefore $5 \times 10^{-3} mol\,dm^{-3}$.

The pH of this base $= 14.0 - (-\log_{10}[OH^-])$
$= 14.0 - (-\log_{10}[5 \times 10^{-3}] = 14.0 - 2.3$
$= 11.7$

5.8 See *table*.

Acid	Base
HNO_3	NO_3^-
H_2SO_3	HSO_3^-
$Fe(H_2O)_6^{3+}$	$Fe(H_2O)_5(OH)^{2+}$
HF	F^-
HNO_2	NO_2^-
$HCOOH$	$HCOO^-$
C_6H_5COOH	$C_6H_5COO^-$
CH_3COOH	CH_3COO^-
C_2H_5COOH	$C_2H_5COO^-$
$Al(H_2O)_6^{3+}$	$Al(H_2O)_5(OH)^{2+}$
$CO_2 + H_2O$	HCO_3^-
$SiO_2 + H_2O$	$HSiO_3^-$
HCO_3^-	CO_3^{2-}
$HSiO_3^-$	SiO_3^{2-}
H_2O	OH^-

5.9 **a** Percentage ionisation = 5.6%

pH = 2.95

b pH = 3.5. Aqueous solutions of aluminium salts are surprisingly acidic. An accidental tipping of aluminium salts into a reservoir in Cornwall created tap-water acidic enough to dissolve copper from pipes and to worry large numbers of people about the possibility of being poisoned.

c pH = 2.4

5.10 *Table 5.3* shows a pK_a value for the dissolving of iron(III) ions, Fe^{3+}, in water between those for sulphurous acid and hydrofluoric acid. Clearly, when iron(III) salts dissolve in water a strongly acidic solution is formed. (You could check this assertion by doing calculations for solutions of different concentrations).

The table supplies data, not reasons for this. The explanation lies in the fact that the iron(III) ions are small and highly positive. They not only attract six water molecules per ion as ligands (see *table 5.3*), they are also able to attract electrons in the O–H bonds of the water molecules themselves.

An electron from an O–H bond in a water molecule is lost to the Fe^{3+} ion, which becomes a hydrated $FeOH^{2+}$ ion. This releases a proton, H^+, which is mopped up by water molecules in solution, making the solution acidic. The small and highly positive Fe^{3+} ion is a proton donor.

$$Fe(H_2O)_6^{3+}(aq) \longrightarrow FeOH(H_2O)_5^{2+}(aq) + H^+(aq)$$

$$H_2O(l) + H^+(aq) \longrightarrow H_3O^+(aq)$$

5.11 Water is the proton donor and is therefore an acid. Its conjugate base is the hydroxide ion, $OH^-(aq)$. The hydride ion, $H^-(aq)$, is a proton acceptor and is therefore a base. Hydrogen, $H_2(g)$, is its conjugate acid.

5.12

Name of base	Base	Conjugate acid
lead hydroxide	$Pb(OH)_2$	$PbOH^+$
silver hydroxide	$AgOH$	Ag^+
ammonia	NH_3	NH_4^+
hydroxylamine	NH_2OH	NH_3OH^+

5.13 Strong acid–strong base: the slope of the graph is steep over the range $pH = 3.5$ to $pH = 10$. Any indicator with a colour-change range within these limits is suitable: bromocresol green, methyl red, bromothymol blue or phenolphthalein. The others in the table are not suitable.

5.14 Strong acid–weak base: the slope is steep over the range 7.0–2.0. The indicators we could use are methyl yellow, methyl orange, bromophenol blue, bromocresol green or methyl red. We might get away with using bromothymol blue, but all the others in the table are unsuitable.

5.15 Weak acid–strong base: methyl orange starts changing colour when the pH is 3.2 and stops at pH 4.4. A large amount of strong base would have to be added to cover this range, so there would be no degree of accuracy.

5.16 a Strong acid–weak base: methyl orange or bromophenol blue.

b Strong acid–strong base: bromocresol green, methyl red, bromothymol blue or phenolphthalein.

c The equilibrium constant for aspirin is similar to that of methanoic acid, so aspirin is a weak acid. Potassium hydroxide is a strong base, so the sensitive region for the indicator would be in the range pH 7–11. Phenolphthalein would be the best choice of indicator.

5.17 Total volume of mixture $= (500 + 500)\,cm^3$
$= 1000\,cm^3 = 1\,dm^3$

The volume of methanoic acid $= 500\,cm^3$
$= 0.5\,dm^3$

The volume of sodium methanoate solution is also $0.5\,dm^3$

$$[HCOOH(aq)] = \frac{0.5\,dm^3 \times 0.1\,mol\,dm^{-3}}{1\,dm^3}$$

$$= 0.05\,mol\,dm^{-3}$$

$$[HCOONa(aq)] = \frac{0.5\,dm^3 \times 0.2\,mol\,dm^{-3}}{1\,dm^3}$$

$$= 0.1\,mol\,dm^{-3}$$

$$[H^+(aq)] = \frac{K_a \times [HCOOH(aq)]}{[HCOONa(aq)]}$$

$$= \frac{1.6 \times 10^{-4} \times 0.05}{0.1}\,mol\,dm^{-3}$$

$$= 8 \times 10^{-5}\,mol\,dm^{-3}$$

pH of the buffer solution
$= -\log_{10}(8 \times 10^{-5}) = 4.1$

This figure is roughly what we would expect, because the pK_a for methanoic acid is 3.8.

b $pH = 4.8$

5.18 Intravenous drugs are those released into the blood stream. This has a pH of around 7.4. If pH was not controlled, blood pH could rise or fall. This could harm the patient, e.g. cause the patient to go into a coma.

5.19 a pH of the benzoic acid/sodium benzoate buffer $= 4.2$

b pH of the ethanoic acid/potassium ethanoate buffer $= 5.7$

c
$$K_b = \frac{[BH^+][OH^-]}{[B]}$$

$$\text{so } [OH^-] = \frac{1.8 \times 10^{-5} \times [B]}{[BH^+]} \text{ mol dm}^{-3}$$

In this case the base B is ammonia and its conjugate acid is the ammonium ion. All you now need to do is to find the concentrations of ammonia and ammonium ion in mol dm^{-3} and substitute in the formula above. Then find the pOH by taking logs, and subtract the answer from 14.0 to find the pH.

The answers are as follows:

$[OH^-] = 9 \times 10^{-6}$ mol dm^{-3}, pOH = 5.0, and pH = 9.0. The latter figure is close to the pK$_a$ of ammonia, i.e. 14.0 − 4.8 = 9.2. This is a useful check.

d pK$_a$ = 10.64

$$K_a = 2.29 \times 10^{-11}$$

$$\text{pH} = 10.25$$

5.20 This kind of problem faces pharmaceutical companies who have to make a cheap reliable product which is safe and stores well – for years in the case of eye-drops. Lemon juice, which contains citric acid, is known to irritate eyes. Other weak acids such as vinegar do the same. Boric acid, already slightly alkaline, is a better bet for a starter, partly because the final solution should also be alkaline. We need a pH lower than 9.2. In the formula

$$[H^+] = \frac{K_a[HA]}{[A^-]} \text{ (see page 80)}$$

we need to have a higher value for [H$^+$] and hence a lower pH. We can do this by making sure that [HA] is bigger than [A$^-$].

One way of doing this is to use equal volumes of different concentrations, e.g. [HA] of 0.1 mol dm^{-3}, and [A$^-$] of 0.01 mol dm^{-3}. Using 0.5 dm^{-3} of each, we can calculate that [H$^+$] = 6.31 × 10^{-9} mol dm^{-3} and the pH = 8.2.

How else can you modify the solution to increase K_a[HA]/[A$^-$]? To get a pH of exactly 7.5, it helps to work back from that pH value and deduce the required concentrations. A spreadsheet and a graph might also be useful. It is up to you!

5.21 a $K_{sp} = [Ag^+][Cl^-]$ **b** $K_{sp} = [Ag^+]^2[S^{2-}]$
c $K_{sp} = [Zn^{2+}][CN^-]^2$

Of the three, silver sulphide is the least soluble in water and silver chloride is the most soluble.

5.22 a For calcium fluoride the units for K_{sp} (= [Ca^{2+}][F$^-$]^2) are the product of three concentrations, each mol dm^{-3}, i.e. mol^3 dm^{-9}. K_{sp} for silver bromide (=[Ag$^+$][Br$^-$]) has for its units the product of two concentrations, giving mol^2 dm^{-6}.

b As the equation for the dissociation of calcium fluoride in water shows, for every calcium ion formed, two fluoride ions form in the same amount of water. So the concentrations of fluoride ion is twice that of the calcium ions.

c Each ion formed makes its own contribution to K_{sp}. For calcium fluoride, K_{sp} = [Ca^{2+}][F$^-$]^2.

d For calcium phosphate, Ca$_3$(PO$_4$)$_2$, K_{sp} = [Ca^{2+}]^3[PO$_4^{3-}$]^2, so the units are (mol dm^{-3})^5 = mol^5 dm^{-15}.

5.23 Using the same method as shown on page 93, [I$^-$] is found to be 3.6 × 10^{-3} mol dm^{-3} when its concentation is tripled, and [Pb^{2+}] is 1.2 × 10^{-3} mol dm^{-3} when its concentration is tripled. The 'ion product'

$$[Pb^{2+}][I^-]^2 = (1.2 \times 10^{-3}) \times (3.6 \times 10^{-3})$$
$$\times (3.6 \times 10^{-3}) \text{ mol}^3 \text{ dm}^{-9}$$
$$= 1.56 \times 10^{-8} \text{ mol}^3 \text{ dm}^{-9}$$

This is greater than K_{sp} for lead iodide (7.1 × 10^{-9} mol^3 dm^{-9}) so there will be a precipitate of lead iodide when the two solutions are mixed.

5.24 You need a soluble salt of silver, e.g. silver nitrate. Adding silver ions to the solution increases their concentration. To keep the solubility product the same (to keep K_{sp} constant) the concentration of chloride ions would have to be reduced. The only practical way this can happen is for the silver chloride to be precipitated, so that chloride ions are removed from the solution.

5.25 **a** Calcium hydroxide contributes calcium ions and hydroxide ions to the solution.

b Sodium hydroxide contributes sodium ions and hydroxide ions to the solution.

c The hydroxide ions are common to both.

d This would cause a decrease in the concentration of calcium ions in solution.

e You would see a precipitate of calcium hydroxide, removing the 'unwanted' calcium ions from the lime water. The precipitate would probably be faint.

5.26 You would need to add either sodium ions or chloride ions from a solution in which the concentration was much greater. An effective (but dangerous) source of chloride ions would be concentrated hydrochloric acid. Adding this slowly to saturated salt solution gives a precipitate of pure salt. This is best done as a demonstration by your teacher.

5.27 In hard tap-water, and even more so in sea-water, there are carbonate ions in solution. If barium carbonate was stirred into either of these two, less of it would dissolve than in pure water. The carbonate ions already in solution would contribute to the solubility product of barium carbonate. Fewer barium ions would be needed in solution, so less barium carbonate would dissolve.

Index (Numbers in italics refer to figures.)